THE BEST OF EPICURE'S

Exciting Vegetarian Cuisines of the World

ASHA KHATAU

Popular Prakashan

www.popularprakashan.com

POPULAR PRAKASHAN PVT. LTD.
301, Mahalaxmi Chambers
22, Bhulabhai Desai Road
Mumbai 400026

First Published 2011
Second Reprint October 2011

(4380)
ISBN 978-81-7991-632-2

Author Photograph on Cover: Mangesh Parab
Food Photography: Arvind Sawant
Cover Design: Mahendra Ghanekar
Design & Typesetting: Namita Jadhav

Printed by
Saurabh Printers Pvt. Ltd.
A-15/16, Sector-IV
Noida - 201 301

Published by
Harsha Bhatkal for
Popular Prakashan Pvt. Ltd.
301, Mahalaxmi Chambers
22, Bhulabhai Desai Road
Mumbai 400026

Dedication

I dedicate this book to my son-in-law Siddharth Singhania whose knowledge of and love for gourmet food has inspired me to create many new recipes.

Author's Note

As the world becomes increasingly vegetarian, it is a challenge for lovers of good food to find enough variety to spice up the daily menu as well as while entertaining. This book is unique for two reasons. One: it contains only vegetarian recipes and two: the recipes are from every corner of the world, that too, using authentic ingredients.

Looking at the overwhelming response to the first volume, I felt that a second volume was long overdue. This volume contains recipes from various international cuisines as in the first volume, but which are more advanced. I have divided them a little differently and added the American section that was missing in the first volume. Each section contains dishes for every course of a meal – starting with soups, salads, appetisers, going on to main dishes and accompaniments and ending with desserts.

The book is divided into six major sections: American, Mexican, Continental, Italian, Mediterranean and Pan Asian. I have not included Indian cuisine, since I have a separate book on it!

Every recipe has been a wonderful culinary journey for me and for the students of my Epicure cooking classes. I hope it is an equally exciting journey of discovery for you. Have fun trying out these tried and tested recipes and delighting friends and family with delicious new surprises. Here's to a truly international experience!

Asha Khatau

Acknowledgements

To the One above, for making me so strong and capable.

Epicure's Vegetarian Cuisines of the World, Volume II is the result of the constant support, encouragement and help of many people.

Firstly my heartfelt thanks to my immediate family. My mother-in-law Leela Khatau for giving me encouragement and support in all I do. I remember my late mother Sudha Sampat for giving me inspiration and courage. I sincerely thank my husband Mahendra Khatau for his constructive suggestions and moral support in whatever I do. How can I forget the help I received from my three children, Priya, Shreya and Manish? I thank them from my heart. My special thanks to Abhaji Singhania for her help and expert touch during the photo shoot. I am grateful to my sister Hina Bhatia and my sister-in law Ameeta Thackersey and brother-in-law Jagdish Thackersey for always being there by my side and helping me in every way. I would also like to thank Vandana Kejriwal and Niti Desai for helping in the photo shoot. I appreciate and thank my dedicated staff Gopinath, Mahadev, Naresh, Dattu and Jha, who are always willing to work and help. I thank everyone on the team of my publisher Popular Prakashan who is associated with this book, for their help and co-operation.

Last but not least, my close friends and my cooking class students receive my sincere vote of thanks, as they are the ones who most eagerly await every new book. I thank them deeply for giving me inspiration to write the recipes, cook them, perfect them and put them together in a book.

Contents

MEDITERRANEAN

MEXICAN

PAN ASIAN

CONTINENTAL

American

American cuisine conjures up visions of burgers, crispy onion rings and French fries. But you will be amazed to discover a tongue-tickling variety of soups, salads and sandwiches including Fiesta Chowder, New Orleans Gumbo, Cajun Red Beans and Rice Salad and Ribbon Sandwiches. And don't forget the feast that awaits you at the Sandwich Bar with its delicious array of breads, spreads and fillings...

Baked Potato Soup

Ingredients

200 gm potatoes, baked in foil

2 tsp butter

1 medium onion, chopped

1 tbsp finely-chopped spring onion

3 cups Vegetable Stock (Page 245)

Salt and pepper to taste

1 cup low-fat cream

To garnish

Sour Cream (Page 245), grated Cheddar cheese, chopped spring onions and parsley

Method

Peel the potatoes and mash lightly with a fork.

Melt the butter in a saucepan; sauté the onion and spring onion until soft. Add the stock, salt, pepper and the mashed potato and stir to blend. Add the cream and heat gently to serving temperature.

Garnish with a dollop of sour cream, grated cheese, spring onion and parsley. Serve hot with crusty bread.

Serves } 4

Pumpkin Soup

Ingredients

1 whole small red pumpkin (700-900 gm)

1 tbsp salad oil or sunflower oil

1 tsp crushed ginger

1 tsp crushed garlic

1 tsp coriander powder

1 medium onion, chopped

1 medium potato, chopped

1 medium carrot, chopped

2 sticks celery, chopped

1½-2 cups Vegetable Stock (Page 245)

Salt, pepper and lemon juice to taste

Chopped coriander leaves, to garnish

To serve

1 small pumpkin shell, cleaned, flesh scooped out and brushed with oil and salt. Reserve the top slice of the pumpkin.

Method

Remove the seeds from the scooped-out pumpkin flesh and chop.

Heat the oil in a large saucepan and add ginger, garlic and coriander powder. Sauté for 2-3 minutes; add all the vegetables and pumpkin and cook until slightly wilted. Add 3 cups of water and transfer the mixture to a pressure cooker and cook till the pressure is released 3 times (3 whistles). Remove from heat and set aside to cool.

Purée the mixture in a blender and pass it through a sieve. Return the soup to the saucepan and heat gently. Add the stock according to the consistency you prefer. Add salt, pepper and lemon juice to taste.

To serve

Bake the empty shell in an oven at 350°F/180°C/Gas Mark 4 for 5-10 minutes. Remove and fill with the soup, cover with the top part of pumpkin and return to the oven. Cook at 400°F/200°C/Gas Mark 6 for 20 minutes.

Garnish with coriander and serve the soup out of the shell. Alternatively you can serve the soup in regular soup bowls with a wedge of lemon.

Serves } 6-8

New Orleans Gumbo

Ingredients

1 tbsp oil

2-3 cloves garlic, crushed

½ cup chopped onions

½ cup chopped red capsicum

250 gm okra, chopped

½ cup boiled green peas

Salt and pepper to taste

1 tsp Tabasco sauce

2-3 bay leaves

1 cup blanched and chopped tomatoes

½ cup tomato juice

2½ cups Vegetable Stock (Page 245)

1 cup cooked rice

To garnish

Chopped fresh parsley

Method

Heat the oil in a saucepan; sauté garlic and onions gently until soft. Add capsicum, okra and peas. Cook for another 5 minutes, stirring occasionally. Add salt, pepper, Tabasco sauce, bay leaves, tomatoes, tomato juice and the stock. Simmer for 5-10 minutes.

Spoon 2-3 tbsp of rice in each bowl, ladle gumbo over the rice and garnish with parsley.

Serves } 4-6

Sandwich Bar
(recipe on page 34)

Fiesta Chowder

Thick Vegetable and Corn Soup

Ingredients

3 tbsp plain flour

1 tbsp Taco seasoning

2 cups mixed vegetables, cubed and boiled

3 tbsp oil

1 medium onion, chopped

1 tsp crushed garlic

1 cup boiled American corn

½ cup black beans, soaked overnight and boiled

1 ½ cups tomatoes, blanched and chopped

2 tbsp finely-chopped jalapeño chillies

¼ cup finely-chopped olives

1 cup boiled brown rice

3 cups water

½ cup (each) grated cheese and milk

Salt and pepper to taste

3 tbsp finely-chopped coriander

To serve

Breadsticks

Method

Combine flour and taco seasoning in a heavy-duty zip-loc plastic bag; add vegetables. Seal and shake to coat. Cook the coated vegetables in hot oil in a large saucepan over high heat, stirring from time to time, for 4 minutes or until browned.

Reduce heat to medium-high; add onion and garlic; sauté for 5 minutes. Add corn, black beans, tomatoes, jalapeño chillies, olives, rice and water. Bring mixture to a boil; reduce heat to low, cover and simmer for 5 minutes. Remove lid and stir in cheese, milk, salt and pepper.

Garnish with coriander and serve with breadsticks.

Serves } 8-10

Lettuce and Apple Salad
(recipe on page 24)

Raspberry Vinaigrette Dressing
(recipe on page 24)

Pumpkin Soup
(recipe on page 15)

Fresh Asparagus Potato Soup

Ingredients

2 tsp olive oil

1 large white onion, peeled and chopped

1 large potato, peeled and cut into 2-inch pieces

4 cups Vegetable Stock (Page 245)

750 gm asparagus, tough bottoms removed and discarded, cut into 1-inch pieces, tips reserved

Salt and freshly-ground pepper to taste

Method

Heat the oil in a heavy saucepan over medium heat. Add the onion and cook, stirring, until it begins to soften. Add the potato and the stock, increase the heat to high, and bring it to a boil. Cover the saucepan, reduce the heat to medium-low and simmer until the potato breaks apart easily when pierced with a fork, about 20 minutes. Add the asparagus and cook for 5 minutes longer.

Transfer the soup to a food processor or blender and process until smooth. Return the soup to the pan; add the asparagus tips, season with salt and pepper to taste, and gently re-heat, allowing the tips to soften.

Serving suggestion: Cut the centre out from a crusty bread round and hollow it. Brush with olive oil and bake in a hot oven to crisp the inside. Use this as a bowl to serve the soup. You will need six 4-inch-wide crusty bread rounds.

Serves } 6

Waldorf Slaw

Ingredients

4 sticks celery, sliced

2 cups shredded red or white cabbage

½ cup chopped and toasted walnuts and raisins

4 stems spring onions, sliced

2 medium green apples, peeled, thinly sliced and tossed in 2 tbsp lemon juice

2 medium carrots, peeled and cut into sticks

For the dressing

4 tbsp Mayonnaise (Page 244)

2 tbsp thick yogurt

2 tbsp vinegar

Salt, pepper and mustard to taste

Method

Combine all the salad ingredients in a bowl and chill.

Whisk together all the ingredients for the dressing and add to the salad. Toss well and transfer to a serving bowl, cover with cling film and chill until ready to serve.

Serves } 4–6

Seven-layer Salad

Ingredients

4 cups salad greens, washed and torn into square pieces

½ cup thinly-sliced celery

½ cup thinly-sliced spring onion

½ cup thinly-sliced red, yellow or green capsicum

200 gm crumbled feta cheese or cottage cheese

1 tbsp freshly-chopped basil

1 cup (each) shelled and boiled green peas and corn kernels

1½ cups Mayonnaise (Page 244)

¾ cup grated Cheddar cheese

Salt and pepper to taste

Method

Place the salad greens in a large glass bowl. Layer celery, spring onion, capsicum, feta cheese mixed with basil, peas and corn over the greens. Spread mayonnaise evenly over the peas and corn, covering the top completely and sealing the edge of the bowl. Sprinkle the cheese and cover the bowl with cling film.

Refrigerate for 2 to 12 hours for the flavours to blend. Toss just before serving and add salt and pepper to taste.

Serves } 6-8

Fresh Asparagus Potato Salad

Ingredients

450 gm potatoes, boiled, peeled, then halved or quartered

250 gm fresh asparagus tips, cut into 2-inch lengths and blanched

½ cup cream, beaten

¾ cup Mayonnaise (Page 244)

¼ cup minced onion

2 cloves garlic, crushed

1 tbsp Dijon mustard

2 tbsp finely-chopped parsley or tarragon

2 tbsp olive oil

1 tbsp tarragon vinegar

Salt and pepper to taste

To garnish

A few lettuce leaves and a small bunch of parsley

Method

Place the potatoes in a bowl and the asparagus tips in another bowl.

In a small bowl, mix together cream, mayonnaise, minced onion, garlic, salt, pepper and mustard. Toss the potatoes in this dressing.

In another small bowl mix together herbs, olive oil, tarragon vinegar, salt and pepper. Toss asparagus tips in this dressing.

Chill both the salads separately. Just before serving, take a flat serving dish, arrange the asparagus tips in the centre in a criss-cross design. Pile up chilled potato salad on top and garnish with a bunch of parsley and lettuce leaves. Serve at once.

Serves } 6

Cajun Red Beans and Rice Salad

Ingredients

1½ cups water

¾ cup long-grain rice

½ tsp salt

1 tbsp chopped thyme + 2 sprigs thyme

200 gm red kidney beans, soaked boiled and drained

1 cup chopped red capsicum

2/3 cup sliced spring onions

1/3 cup olive oil

3 tbsp white wine vinegar

2 tbsp Cajun Seasoning Mix (recipe follows)

Salt and pepper to taste

Method

Bring 1½ cups water to boil in a small saucepan. Stir in rice, ½ tsp salt and a sprig of thyme; return to heat and bring to a boil. Reduce heat to low; cover and cook for about 20 minutes until liquid is absorbed and rice is tender.

Transfer rice to a large bowl and remove the sprig of thyme. Cool for 5 minutes. Stir beans, capsicum and spring onions into the rice. Add oil, vinegar, Cajun seasoning, and chopped thyme and mix well. Season salad with salt and pepper to taste. Garnish with remaining sprig of thyme and serve.

Serves } 4-6

Cajun Seasoning Mix

Mix together 1 tbsp garlic powder, 1 tbsp onion powder, 2 tsp black or white pepper powder, 2 tsp dried thyme, ½ tsp dried oregano, and 1½ tsp chilli flakes. Fill in an airtight bottle and use as required.

Makes 4 tbsp

Traditional Cole Slaw

Ingredients

450 gm white cabbage, shredded

2 carrots, grated

2 sticks celery, trimmed

1 small green capsicum, sliced long

5-6 tbsp Mayonnaise (Page 244)

1 level tsp sugar

½ tsp salt

½ tsp pepper powder

½ tsp lemon juice

1 tbsp onion, finely chopped

Method

Place the vegetables in a large salad bowl. Mix together mayonnaise, sugar, salt, pepper, lemon juice and finely-chopped onion. Add this dressing to the vegetables and toss well. Chill before serving.

Serves } 4-6

Lettuce and Apple Salad

with Raspberry Vinaigrette Dressing

Ingredients

5 cups chopped mixed lettuce greens

1 medium green apple, thinly sliced

2 tbsp lemon juice

¼ cup (each) dried cranberries, chopped walnuts and pumpkin seeds

For raspberry vinaigrette

⅓ cup (each) olive oil or salad oil and raspberry preserve

¼ cup wine vinegar or raspberry vinegar

1 tbsp (each) lemon juice and Dijon mustard

1 tsp dried herbs

Salt and pepper to taste

Method

Wash and soak lettuce leaves in ice-cold water. Rinse and completely dry the leaves in a strainer or pass through salad spinner. Transfer to a serving bowl,

Rub apple slices with lemon juice and place in a bowl over lettuce leaves. Cover with cling wrap and keep cold. In a small bowl, mix together cranberries, walnuts and pumpkin seeds. Set aside.

For the vinaigrette
Mix all the ingredients for the vinaigrette in a screw-top jar and shake thoroughly to mix well.

To serve
Just before serving, sprinkle nuts over the salad, pour vinaigrette all over and toss the salad with salad tongs starting from below and going upwards. Serve immediately.

Serves } 6

Crunchy Vegetable Wraps

with Buttermilk or Ranch Dressing

Ingredients

4 Wholewheat Tortillas (recipe follows)

1 cup alfalfa sprouts (optional)

1 cup shredded cabbage

½ cup finely-chopped tomato

¼ cup cottage cheese, crumbled

2 tbsp finely-chopped spring onion

2 tbsp finely-chopped basil leaves

Salt and pepper to taste

1 tbsp mustard paste

½ tbsp balsamic vinegar

¼ cup cream cheese

4 large heads curly leaf lettuce

To serve

Buttermilk or ranch dressing

Note: If you want to serve this as an appetiser, roll each tortilla like a Swiss roll and cut it into three parts. Serve chilled.

Method

In a medium-sized bowl, mix together alfalfa sprouts (if using), cabbage, tomato, crumbled cottage cheese, spring onion and basil leaves. Season with salt and pepper. Drizzle balsamic vinegar and toss gently to mix. Chill in a refrigerator for half an hour.

When ready to serve, divide the vegetable mixture into four equal portions. Mix mustard and cream cheese in a small bowl and spread evenly on each tortilla, press one curly leaf lettuce on it, and place a portion of vegetable mixture over the leaf. Roll each tortilla into a cone and place upright in a glass. Serve with buttermilk or ranch dressing.

Serves } 4

Wholewheat Tortillas

Mix together 1 cup wholewheat flour, ¼ tsp salt, ¼ tsp baking powder and ¼ cup warm water and make soft dough. Divide into 4 portions. Roll out each one into a thin tortilla and roast on a hot griddle, turning over to cook both sides. Cover and set aside.

Makes 4 tortillas

Ribbon Sandwiches

Ingredients

1 unsliced loaf of white bread

1 unsliced loaf of brown bread

100 gm butter

2-3 tbsp finely-chopped mixed herbs (such as parsley, basil, chives)

Garlic salt and pepper to taste

4-5 tbsp Mayonnaise (Page 244)

4-5 tbsp grated Parmesan cheese

2-3 tbsp finely-chopped red capsicum

½ cup crumbled cottage cheese

¼ cup finely-chopped olives

¼ cup finely-chopped tomatoes

Method

Cut each loaf horizontally into three half-inch-thick slices.

In a bowl, mix together the butter, herbs, salt and pepper. Set aside.

In another bowl, mix together mayonnaise, Parmesan cheese and capsicum.

In a third bowl, mix crumbled cottage cheese, olives and tomatoes.

Place the first slice on a plate and spread herbed butter evenly on it. Top with mayonnaise-cheese-capsicum filling. Cover with another slice of bread and butter this as well. Spread the cottage cheese mixture evenly over it. Repeat the layers once more, finishing with a bread slice. You will get two such loaves. Cover them with a damp cloth and refrigerate for 1-2 hours. To serve, cut the loaves vertically into half inch-thick slices and then cut each slice diagonally in half.

Makes 30 slices

Crispy Onion Rings

Ingredients

2-3 medium onions cut into ¼-inch-thick slices

½ cup plain flour

¼ cup cornflour

Salt and paprika to taste

2 tbsp mashed potatoes

1 cup cold club soda

2 cups toasted breadcrumbs

Oil for deep-frying

Method

Separate the onion leaves and set aside.

Sieve the flour, cornflour, paprika and salt. Make a smooth batter by adding mashed potato and club soda; mix well and set aside in the refrigerator for 10 minutes.

Heat the oil. Transfer breadcrumbs onto a shallow plate. Remove the batter from the fridge and check the consistency; it should be like pancake batter. You can add more club soda if the mixture is too thick. Spear each onion ring with a fork, dip it in the batter, coating it well and shaking off the excess batter. Now dip in the breadcrumbs and fry a few rings at a time until golden; drain on a paper towel and serve immediately.

Serves } 4

Vegetable Burger

Ingredients

6 large burger buns cut horizontally into half
2 tbsp butter, at room temperature
6 cheese slices
6 Vegetable Cutlets (recipe follows)
Cole Slaw for 6 burgers (recipe follows)

For vegetable cutlets

3 medium onions, finely chopped
6-8 cloves garlic, finely chopped
4-5 green chillies, finely chopped (optional)
2 cups mashed potatoes
2 cups mixed vegetables, finely chopped and boiled
1 tbsp lemon juice
Salt, pepper and mustard to taste
3 slices bread, fried crisp and powdered
Breadcrumbs to roll
Oil for frying

For cole slaw

5-6 tbsp Mayonnaise (Page 244)
1 level tsp sugar
½ tsp each salt and pepper
½ tsp lemon juice
1 tbsp onion, finely chopped
450 gm white cabbage, shredded
2 carrots, grated
2 sticks celery, trimmed
1 small green capsicum, sliced long

To serve

French fries, tomato ketchup and mustard paste

Method

For the cutlets

Heat 1 tbsp of oil in a frying pan, fry onion, garlic and chillies (if using) until soft. In a bowl, mix together mashed potatoes, boiled vegetables and lemon juice. Add onion mixture, salt, pepper, mustard and breadcrumbs. Mix well. Divide the mixture into 6 parts and shape them into round patties matching the size of burger buns. Roll each one in breadcrumbs and shallow-fry them in a little oil. Set aside.

For the cole slaw

Mix together mayonnaise, sugar, salt, pepper, lemon juice and finely-chopped onion. Place the vegetables in a large salad bowl, add dressing and toss well. Chill.

To assemble

Brush the bun halves with butter and warm them slightly. Place a cheese slice on the base of the bun. Heat in the oven until cheese melts. Place a hot cutlet on the cheese slice and top it with ¼ cup of cole slaw. Cover with the other half of the bun and gently press it down. Serve immediately with French fries, tomato ketchup and mustard paste.

Makes 6 burgers

Submarine Sandwich

Ingredients

Two 6 inch-long or one 12 inch-long Italian bread loaves/loaf, halved horizontally

¼ cup (each) Mayonnaise (Page 244) and cream cheese

Salt, pepper and mustard to taste

2-3 large iceberg or romaine lettuce leaves, washed

1 medium onion, thinly sliced

2 medium tomatoes, sliced

3-4 pieces pickled gherkins, sliced

½ cup alfalfa sprouts

4 cheese slices or ½ cup grated cheese

To serve

Tomato ketchup, Mayonnaise (Page 244), chilli sauce and mustard paste

Method

Scoop out some breadcrumbs from the cut bread.

In a small bowl, mix together breadcrumbs, mayonnaise, cream cheese, salt, pepper and mustard. Mix well. Spread this evenly on both sides of the bread. Layer the base with lettuce, onion, tomatoes, gherkins, alfalfa sprouts and cheese. Gently press the top part over and serve with tomato ketchup, mayonnaise, chilli sauce and mustard paste.

Serves } 2

Some additional sauces make the sub interesting.

Chipotle Sauce

Ingredients

½ medium onion, chopped

1 tbsp olive oil

1 clove garlic, minced

200 gm tomato purée

1 cup Vegetable Stock (Page 245)

2 chipotle chillies, minced

Method

Sauté onion in oil until soft. Add remaining ingredients and simmer for 20 minutes. Cool and bottle.

Caesar Sauce

Ingredients

4 tbsp Mayonnaise (Page 244)

1 clove garlic, crushed

Juice and zest of 1 lemon

½ cup grated Parmesan cheese

2 tsp Worcestershire sauce

1 tsp Dijon mustard

1 tsp coarse black pepper

3 tbsp extra-virgin olive oil

Method

Place mayonnaise, garlic, lemon, cheese, sauce, mustard and pepper in a small blender jar and turn it on. Stream the olive oil into the dressing through centre of the lid. When the oil is combined, transfer the dressing with a spatula into a bowl or fill it in a jar.

Sweet Onion Sauce

Ingredients

½ cup light corn syrup

1 tbsp minced onion

1 tbsp red wine vinegar

2 tsp cider vinegar

1 tsp balsamic vinegar and brown sugar

¼ tsp lemon juice

A pinch of poppy seeds and salt

A pinch of coarse black pepper and garlic powder

Method

Combine all ingredients in a small microwave-safe bowl. Heat mixture uncovered in the microwave for 1 to 1½ minutes on high until mixture boils. Mix well, cover and cool. Alternatively, bring to a boil on top of stove. Cool and transfer to a serving bowl.

Thousand Island Sauce

Blend together ½ cup Mayonnaise (Page 244), 3 tbsp tomato ketchup, 1 tbsp each of minced onion, grated green capsicum, chopped green olives, 1 tbsp each of sweet pickle and vinegar and 1 tsp sugar, salt and pepper to taste.

Honey Mustard Sauce

Blend together ¼ cup honey with 2 tbsp Dijon mustard. Store in a jar.

Loaded Baked Potato Skins

Ingredients

6-8 medium-sized potatoes

1 tbsp olive oil

½ cup (each) grated cheese and boiled corn

¼ cup (each) finely-chopped red capsicum and spring onion

Salt, pepper and paprika to taste

To garnish

Finely-chopped parsley

To serve

Sour Cream (Page 245)

Method

Wash, pat dry the potatoes and wrap tightly in foil. Bake in an oven at 350°F/180°C/Gas Mark 4 for 15-20 minutes. Remove from foil and cut into half vertically from the centre. With a small spoon, scoop out a little of potato pulp, leaving the shell intact. Brush the skins with olive oil and bake again until slightly brown (approx. 7-8 minutes).

In a small bowl, mix together the cheese, corn, capsicum, spring onion, salt, pepper and paprika. Stuff this mixture into the hollowed potato skins. Bake again in preheated oven until cheese has melted and the top is golden brown. Remove from oven, transfer to a serving plate, garnish with parsley and serve hot with sour cream.

Serves } 6

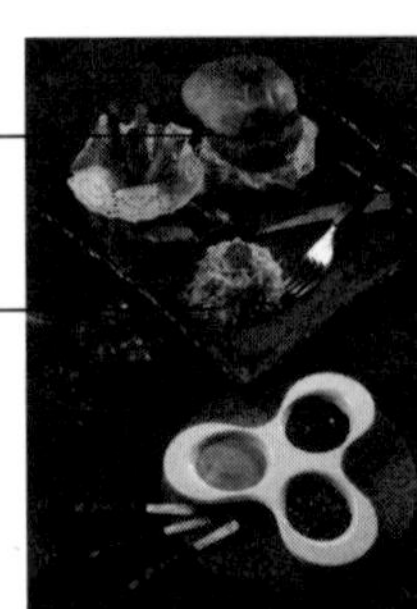

Vegetable Burger (recipe on page 28)

Traditional Cole Slaw (recipe on page 23)

Broccoli and Rice Casserole

Ingredients

2 tbsp butter

1 cup chopped fresh mushrooms

½ cup chopped onion

2 cloves garlic, minced

1 tin (500 gm) cream soup of your choice

½ cup grated Cheddar cheese

2 cups cooked long-grain rice

½ cup red kidney beans, soaked overnight and boiled

500 gm broccoli, stemmed, washed and boiled

or

250 gm artichoke hearts, drained and chopped

½ cup Sour Cream (Page 245)

1 tbsp taco seasoning or chilli flakes

Salt and pepper to taste

Oil to grease the dish

To garnish

Grated cheese and chopped parsley and basil

Method

Melt butter over high heat; add chopped mushrooms. Cook and stir for about 2 minutes. Add onion. Stir in garlic and cook for about a minute longer. Add undiluted tinned soup and the cheese. Stir until cheese is melted. Remove from heat and add cooked rice, beans, broccoli or artichoke, sour cream, taco seasoning, salt and pepper.

Spoon the mixture into a greased casserole dish. Spread grated cheese over and bake for 20 minutes at 350°F/180°C/Gas Mark 4. Garnish with parsley and basil and serve hot.

Serves } 8

Crispy Onion Rings (recipe on page 27)

Loaded Baked Potato Skins (recipe on page 32)

Sandwich Bar

Welcome to the sandwich bar. Here is a selection of breads, fillings, sauces and seasonings. Enjoy assembling, grilling, toasting and serving!

Assorted Breads

1. White and brown sandwich bread, squares or triangles
2. Pita bread, oval or round; white or brown
3. Bagels
4. Focaccia
5. French bread (*baguette*)
6. Indian *laadi* pav or burger buns
7. Wholewheat, 7-grain, 3-grain or rye bread
8. Ciabatta or sour dough bread
9. Multi-grain bread
10. Croissants

Assorted Spreads

1. Spinach, pesto and cream cheese spread: Blend together ½ cup cream cheese spread, ¼ cup grated Parmesan cheese, 2 tbsp Pesto Sauce (Page 75), 4 tbsp blanched spinach and 1 tsp lemon juice.

2. Mexican chilli spread: Mix 100 gm each of grated Monterey Jack cheese and cream cheese spread, with 2 tbsp chopped jalapeño chillies and ½ tsp taco seasoning.

3. Honey-mustard spread: Beat ¼ cup of butter with 1 tbsp honey, 2 tbsp Dijon mustard and 1 tbsp toasted sesame seeds.

4. Sandwich spread: Blend together 1 small grated onion, 1 large clove garlic, 100 gm grated Cheddar cheese, 1 tbsp tomato purée, ½ tbsp mustard, 3-4 pieces each pickled capers and gherkins, dash of Tabasco, salt and pepper to taste. Transfer to a bowl and fold in ½ cup of Mayonnaise (Page 244). Fill in a jar and refrigerate.

5. Olive spread: Grind 200 gm green or black olives, 2 tbsp pine nuts or walnuts, 2 tbsp capers, 1 tsp dried oregano, 1 large clove garlic, ½ tsp lemon juice, 2 tbsp extra-virgin olive oil, a pinch of chilli flakes, salt and pepper in a blender jar or food processor to a coarse texture. Adjust seasoning and store in a jar.

6. Tofu spread: Blend 200 gm tofu with 200 gm thick yogurt, salt, 1 tbsp each of vinegar and sugar. You can add 1 tbsp of freshly-chopped mixed herbs or 3-4 crushed cloves garlic.
7. Sun-dried tomato spread: Process together 50 gm sun-dried tomatoes (soaked in hot water for 15 minutes), 2 cloves garlic, ¼ cup each of Parmesan cheese and blanched almonds, 1 tbsp each of parsley and basil, 1 tsp balsamic vinegar, grated rind of 1 lemon, salt and pepper in a blender. Slowly pour ¼ cup olive oil into the mixture. Blend until the mixture is a smooth paste. Makes 2 cups.
8. Wasabi cream: Combine 1-2 tbsp wasabi powder with 1 tbsp lemon juice in a bowl until smooth. Leave to stand for 5 minutes. Add 1 cup Mayonnaise (Page 244) and whisk to combine. Refrigerate until ready to use.
9. Cream cheese and dill spread: Blend together ½ cup cream cheese spread with 2 tbsp chopped dill, 1 tsp Dijon mustard, 1 clove garlic, 1 tsp lemon juice, ½ tsp each of salt and pepper until smooth. Remove from the blender jar and fold in ¼ cup thick yogurt and chill.
10. Herbed hummus: Blend together 150 gm soaked and boiled chickpeas, 2 tbsp each of tahina paste and lemon juice, 3-4 cloves garlic, salt to taste and 1 tbsp chopped parsley and basil. Garnish with olive oil and chilli flakes.

Assorted Fillings

1. Grilled vegetables such as red and yellow capsicums, zucchini, baby corn, onions, asparagus etc. tossed with olive oil, balsamic vinegar, Italian seasoning, salt and pepper.
2. Crunchy vegetable fillings such as salad greens, alfalfa sprouts, sliced olives, grated carrots and shredded cabbage, chopped fresh herbs, finely-chopped apples and walnuts. In a small bowl mix together 2 tbsp olive oil, 1 tbsp each of balsamic vinegar, 2 crushed cloves garlic, 1 tbsp finely-chopped tarragon, 1 tsp each of mustard, salt, pepper and Worcestershire sauce. Toss the salad with this dressing.
3. 200 gm crumbled cottage cheese, mixed with ¼ cup each of finely-chopped red capsicum, spring onion, tomato and carrot and 1 tbsp chopped basil. Season with salt, pepper and paprika.
4. 1 cup boiled potato, ¼ cup spring onion and 2 tbsp chopped walnuts, tossed with herbed mayonnaise. Season with salt, pepper and mustard.
5. 200 gm roasted eggplant cubes, tossed with ½ cup thick yogurt, 2-3 cloves crushed garlic, 1 tsp each of lemon juice and chopped dill, 2-3 tbsp olive oil and salt to taste.
6. Mozzarella and tomato slices marinated in olive oil, crushed garlic, chopped fresh basil, salt and pepper.

7. Chopped salad leaves, tomato wedges, sliced olives, sliced cucumber, feta cheese cubes, tossed with olive oil, cider vinegar, salt, pepper, mustard, dried herbs and sugar.
8. Caramelised onions, slivers of sun-dried tomatoes and Emmental or Gouda cheese.
9. Combine 1 cup of freshly-chopped tender spinach leaves with 1 tbsp each of grated radish, ginger and toasted sesame seeds. Toss with wasabi cream and use it as a filling for steamed bread or multi-grain bread.

Additional ingredients

1. Herbed butter
2. Cheese slices
3. Tomato slices
4. Mustard
5. Salt, pepper, paprika
6. Olive oil flavoured with garlic and herbs
7. Slivers of Parmesan cheese
8. Jalapeño chilli slices
9. Tomato ketchup

Ciabatta Sandwich

Ingredients

½ cup green or black olive tapenade

3 tbsp Italian vinaigrette dressing

1 loaf ciabatta bread, sliced horizontally

8 lettuce leaves

8 cheese slices

8 tomato slices

Method

Combine tapenade and Italian dressing in a small bowl and spread the mixture on the cut side of the bread. Layer the bottom half of bread with 4 lettuce leaves, cheese, tomatoes and remaining lettuce leaves. Cover with the top half of bread. Secure with toothpicks. Cut into 8 pieces and serve.

Makes 8 sandwiches

Toasted Bagel Sandwich

Ingredients

Butter

2 bagels cut horizontally

Cream cheese spread

Grainy mustard to spread

Tomato slices

Iceberg or arugula lettuce

Slivers of fresh Parmesan cheese

Method

Spread a little butter on the cut sides of the bagel and lightly toast the breads in a grill or toaster. Leave to cool slightly. Spread the cream cheese and mustard. Stack tomato, lettuce and slivers of Parmesan. Cover with the other piece of bread and serve.

Serves } 2

Mediterranean Delight

Ingredients

2 six-inch round pita breads, slit to make pockets

½ cup Hummus (Page 101)

½ cup grilled vegetables or crunchy vegetable salad (see Assorted Fillings)

Olive oil and balsamic dressing

Salt and pepper to taste

Method

Line the inside of the pita pockets with hummus. Toss the salad or the grilled vegetables in the olive oil and balsamic dressing. Season it with salt and pepper. Spoon the mixture into the hummus-lined pita pockets. Serve immediately.

Serves } 2

Cottage Cheese and Vegetable Sandwich

Ingredients

8 slices brown or wholewheat bread

1 tbsp olive oil

1 tbsp low-fat butter

1 tbsp finely-chopped basil

1 tbsp finely-chopped chives

1 tsp garlic salt

1 tsp mustard

1 tsp pepper

1 cup each finely-grated carrot, onions and capsicum

¼ cup each thick yogurt and cottage cheese, mixed together

To garnish

Sliced tomatoes, olive oil and chilli flakes

Method

Remove the crust from the bread slices and cut into half to make triangles. Wrap in a damp cloth and set aside. In a bowl, mix together oil, butter, basil, chives, garlic salt, mustard and pepper. Mix well. Add all the vegetables, yogurt and cottage cheese. Divide the mixture into 4 parts. Spread evenly on four slices of bread. Cover with the remaining slices and press down lightly. Cut each one into half and arrange on a serving plate. Cut tomato slices into half and place each half on the halved sandwiches. Drizzle a little olive oil, sprinkle chilli flakes on top and serve.

Serves } 4

Corn and Cheese Grilled Sandwich

Ingredients

2-3 tbsp butter

8 slices brown or white sandwich bread

1 cup boiled corn kernels

1 cup grated Monterey Jack cheese

2-3 pieces jalapeño chillies, finely chopped

2 tbsp Red Salsa (Page 135)

Salt, pepper and taco seasoning to taste

Method

Spread butter lightly on all the slices of bread. Mix remaining ingredients in a bowl. Divide the mixture equally amongst 4 slices, cover with remaining slices and press lightly. Spread a little butter on the top and bottom of the sandwiches and grill until crisp. Serve hot.

Makes 4 sandwiches

Mushroom and Onion Open Sandwich

Ingredients

1 tbsp butter

1 tbsp olive oil

2 cloves garlic, crushed

2 medium onions, finely chopped

250 gm fresh button mushrooms, washed and sliced

2 tbsp fresh cream

1 tbsp chopped parsley

Salt and pepper to taste

8-10 slices of French bread (*baguette*)

Grated Cheddar cheese or 4-5 cheese slices

Method

In a frying pan, heat butter and oil together. Sauté the garlic and onions till transparent. Add the mushrooms and cook until the mixture is dry. Add cream, parsley, salt and pepper. Cook for a minute, remove from heat and set aside to cool. Toast the bread lightly and spread the mixture evenly on the toast. Sprinkle cheese and place under a hot grill until the cheese melts. Serve immediately.

Makes 8-10 open sandwiches

Italian

What is that special quality that makes Italian cuisine so universally loved? Some may say it is the liberal use of olive oil; others may point to the bewildering variety of pasta – spaghetti, macaroni, fusilli and lasagna; while pizza may be the defining Italian dish for some! Savour perennial Italian favourites like Chunky Pizza Soup, Potato Pie, Tortellini, Ravioli and an amazing Chilli Risotto with Mushrooms and Balsamic Reduction.

Creamy Minestrone Soup

Ingredients

¼ cup dried white beans, soaked and boiled

2 tbsp butter

2 cups finely-chopped and boiled mixed vegetables (carrots, French beans, potatoes, onions, peas and zucchini)

4 cups Vegetable Stock (Page 245)

1 bay leaf

1 cup whole milk

1 tsp salt

Freshly ground pepper to taste

To garnish

1 tbsp chopped garlic

1 tbsp finely-chopped basil

1 tbsp finely-chopped parsley

1 tbsp grated Parmesan cheese

Method

Melt butter in a large saucepan; sauté the vegetables and beans for one minute. Add bay leaf, stock, salt and pepper. Bring to a boil and simmer for 3-4 minutes.

Just before serving, add milk, garnish with garlic, basil, parsley and cheese. Serve hot.

Serves } 6

Popcorn Soup

Ingredients

2 tbsp butter

1 tin (350 gm) cream-style corn

½ cup yellow corn kernels, boiled

1 medium onion, finely chopped

1 clove garlic, finely chopped

½ green capsicum, finely chopped

2 cups Vegetable Stock (Page 245)

1 cup milk+1 tsp cornflour, blended

Salt and pepper to taste

To garnish

1 tbsp parsley, finely chopped

1 cup popped corn

Method

Melt butter in a heavy saucepan and sauté the onion, garlic and capsicum until soft. Add the corn kernels. Combine the cream-style corn and stock and add to the pan. Continue stirring and season with salt and pepper. Simmer the soup for 10-15 minutes. Add the milk and cornflour mixture.

Ladle the soup into individual bowls and garnish with parsley and 6-7 pieces of popped corn in each bowl.

Serves } 4-6

Chunky Pizza Soup

Ingredients

1 medium onion, finely chopped

½ cup (each) sliced mushrooms and green capsicum

½ cup grated pizza cheese tossed with 1 tsp plain flour

1 cup (each) coarsely chopped blanched tomatoes and Vegetable Stock (Page 245)

1 tbsp (each) finely-chopped basil, olive oil and pizza seasoning

Salt and pepper to taste

To serve

Pizza base, toasted with olive oil and Italian seasoning

Method

Preheat the oven to 350°F/180°C/Gas mark 4.

Heat oil over medium heat and stir fry onion, mushrooms and capsicum until soft. Do not brown them. Add the tomatoes, stock, salt, pepper, pizza seasoning and basil. Cook till heated through.

Ladle the soup into an ovenproof bowl and sprinkle with cheese. Bake in the preheated oven till the cheese melts and is bubbly. Serve right away with toasted and seasoned pizza base.

Serves } 4

Note: You can broil this soup in individual bowls as well.

Tomato Asparagus Soup

Ingredients

For the tomato soup

4 medium tomatoes, diced

1 medium onion, diced

2 tbsp olive oil

2 cloves garlic, chopped

2 tbsp tomato purée

4 cups water

Salt and pepper to taste

For the asparagus soup

200 gm fresh asparagus

2 tbsp olive oil

1 (each) onion, potato and leek, diced

½ bundle (125 gm) spinach leaves, chopped

4 cups water

Salt and pepper to taste

To garnish

2-3 cooked asparagus tips and a bunch of celery leaves

Method

For the tomato soup

Heat oil in a saucepan and sauté the onion, garlic and tomatoes. Cook until soft. Add the tomato purée and water. Simmer for 10-15 minutes. Add salt and pepper. Blend in a liquidizer, sieve and set aside.

For the asparagus soup

Cook the asparagus in salted boiling water for 7-8 minutes. Trim 2-3 tips to 4-5 inches length and set aside. Heat the oil in a saucepan and sauté the onion and leek together. Add the asparagus, spinach, potato, salt, pepper and water. Cook for 20 minutes. Blend the mixture in liquidizer, sieve and set aside.

To serve

Pour the tomato soup in a bowl till half full. Then place a spatula at the edge of the bowl, pour the asparagus soup from over the spatula, and move the spatula towards the middle of the bowl. Garnish with asparagus tips and celery leaves.

Serves } 4

Vegetable Soup with Basil Sauce

Ingredients

For the soup

2 tbsp olive oil

1 medium (each) potato and zucchini, cut into small cubes

2 medium tomatoes, blanched and chopped

½ cup (each) boiled peas, boiled pasta and soaked and boiled broad beans

5 cups Vegetable Stock (Page 245)

Salt and pepper to taste

For basil sauce

½ cup fresh basil leaves

2 large cloves garlic

½ tsp (each) salt and pepper

3 tbsp Parmesan cheese

⅓ cup olive oil

Method

For the soup

Heat olive oil in a saucepan and add potato and zucchini. Cook for 3-4 minutes. Add peas, beans and tomatoes along with stock, salt and pepper. Boil for 3-4 minutes, add the pasta and remove from stove.

For basil sauce

Blend all the ingredients except oil in a small blender jar for 20 seconds. Gradually add oil until smooth. Refrigerate until needed.

Pour hot soup in individual bowls, spoon basil sauce on top and serve.

Serves } 6

Italian Pizza Salad

Ingredients

200 gm uncooked wagon wheel or shell-shaped pasta

½ cup cherry tomatoes, halved

½ cup (each) sliced spring onion, olive and capsicum

½ cup pizza cheese, cut into cubes

½ tsp (each) Italian seasoning and chilli flakes

¼ tsp freshly-ground pepper

For the dressing

4 tbsp freshly-chopped basil

1 large clove garlic, minced

2 tbsp grated Parmesan cheese

4 tbsp olive oil

2 tbsp lemon juice

Salt and pepper to taste

Method

Boil the pasta for 8-10 minutes, drain and set aside. To make the dressing mix all the ingredients in a small bowl and whisk until well blended. Pour this over the pasta and toss. Add the remaining salad ingredients and toss again. Cover and refrigerate for 2-3 hours. Serve cold.

Serves } 6

Antipasto Salad with Garlic Dressing

Ingredients

4 tbsp (each) white and black beans, soaked and boiled

½ cup (each) roasted red capsicum and eggplant, cubed

¼ cup sliced black olives

1 cup blanched and coarsely chopped tomatoes

2 medium onions, chopped

½ cup mozzarella cheese, cubed

1 medium zucchini, sliced and grilled

3-4 tbsp olive oil

Garlic dressing

2 tbsp olive oil

1 tbsp (each) balsamic vinegar and finely-chopped tarragon

1 tsp (each) mustard, salt, pepper and Worcestershire sauce

2 cloves garlic, crushed

Method

Heat olive oil in a thick frying pan and sauté the onions until soft. Add the beans and tomatoes. Cook until extra water from tomatoes evaporates. Add capsicum, eggplant, zucchini and olives. Mix well. Remove from stove and add set aside to cool slightly. Add the cheese and the dressing. Adjust the seasoning. Toss gently to mix. Serve at room temperature or cold.

For the dressing
Place all the ingredients in a screw-top jar and shake well. Use as required.

Serves } 4-6

Creamy Minestrone Soup
(recipe on page 42)

See Continental Section
Corn and Potato Rösti
(recipe on page 229)

Spinach and Cottage Cheese Bread Bowl
(recipe on page 233)

1DL/DECILITER

Tuscan Salad

Ingredients

1½ cups long grain rice, cooked

¼ cup white wine or Vegetable Stock (Page 245)

1 red capsicum, thinly sliced

1 yellow capsicum, thinly sliced

3 tbsp fagioli (small white beans), soaked and boiled

8-10 olives, halved

2 stems spring onions, thinly sliced

1 medium tomato, quartered

1 small iceberg lettuce, torn into square pieces

For the dressing

1 tsp salt

1 tsp pepper

1 tsp Tabasco

1 tsp chopped garlic

3 tbsp grainy mustard

1 cup Mayonnaise (Page 244)

⅓ cup brown vinegar

3 tbsp Worcestershire sauce

4 tbsp Parmesan cheese

Method

Place cooked rice in a bowl and pour stock or wine over it while the rice is hot. Set aside to cool. Add the rest of the vegetables and beans and toss gently to mix. Cover the bowl with cling film and chill until ready to use.

For the dressing
Place all the ingredients in a blender and blend to mix.

Just before serving, pour the dressing over the salad, toss gently and serve at once.

Serves } 6

Traditional Pizza
(recipe on page 55)

Panini

Italian-style Sandwich

Ingredients

4 oblong flat bread loaves, halved and lightly buttered

8 slices mozzarella cheese

2 medium tomatoes, sliced

2 tsp dried oregano and basil mixed

Garlic-flavoured olive oil

Salt and pepper to taste

Method

Layer the bread slices with mozzarella, tomatoes and herbs. Drizzle olive oil and sprinkle salt and pepper over. Serve cold or sandwich and grill.

Makes 8 appetizer portions

Variations for topping:

1. Sliced olives, onions, mozzarella cheese and herbs
2. Lettuce, cucumber, tomato, chives and balsamic vinegar
3. Mozzarella, cooked asparagus tips, chives and lemon juice
4. Melted mozzarella slice, tomato slice and chopped basil leaves
5. Boiled corn, pepper, onion and cheese

Caprese Salad Appetiser

Ingredients

3 large firm red tomatoes cut into ¼-inch thick slices

200 gm fresh mozzarella cheese cut into ¼-inch thick slices

¼ cup extra-virgin olive oil

1 tbsp balsamic vinegar

1 large clove garlic, minced

Salt and pepper to taste

12-14 fresh basil leaves

To garnish

A small bunch of basil

To serve

10-12 quarter-inch thick slices of toasted crusty bread

Method

Arrange tomato slices in an ovenproof glass dish. Cover each tomato slice with a slice of mozzarella.

In a small bowl, mix olive oil, balsamic vinegar, garlic, salt and pepper. Drizzle this mixture over the tomato-mozzarella slices.

Just before serving, place under a hot grill for 1-2 minutes. Remove and place basil leaves on the cheese. Place each slice of tomato and cheese on a slice of toasted bread and serve immediately.

Makes 12 appetisers

Panzarotti

Fried, Stuffed Pasta

Ingredients

For the dough

1 1/4 cups plain flour, sieved

1 1/2 tbsp butter

A pinch of salt

Cold water to make the dough

Oil for frying

For the filling

200 gm Ricotta Cheese (recipe follows), crumbled

100 gm mozzarella cheese, grated

100 gm Parmesan cheese, grated

1/2 cup green capsicum, diced

or

1/2 cup thinly-chopped spinach

1 tbsp finely-chopped parsley

2 tbsp cream

Salt, pepper and nutmeg to taste

Method

For the dough

Make a soft dough with all the ingredients and set aside for 1 hour.

For the filling

In a medium bowl, combine ricotta with cream, salt, pepper and nutmeg. Beat until creamy. In another small bowl, mix together mozzarella and Parmesan cheeses along with capsicum or spinach and parsley. Fold this into ricotta mixture.

To make panzarotti

Roll out the dough and cut into rectangular strips wide enough to be cut out into 3-inch circles. Dust each one with a little flour. Place each circle on your palm and spoon a little mixture in the centre. Fold the edge over to make a half-moon shape. Press the edges lightly. Just before serving, deep-fry in hot oil and serve immediately.

Makes 18-20 pieces

Ricotta Cheese

Heat 1 litre of milk mixed with 250 gm of fresh cream. When it comes to a boil, add 2 tbsp white vinegar and 1 tbsp salt. When it begins to bubble, remove from the heat. Lift all the cheese which floats up to the top with a slotted spoon and drain completely through a piece of muslin. When completely cooled, cut into cubes and store with a little liquid from the cheese in an airtight box.

Makes 300 gm

Olive and Sun-dried Tomato Crostini

Ingredients

16 slices crusty bread

¼ cup olive oil

⅓ cup black or green olives, sliced

⅓ cup sun-dried tomatoes

200 grams mozzarella cheese

¼ teaspoon salt

¼ teaspoon pepper

1 tablespoon freshly-chopped basil and parsley

To garnish

Freshly-chopped basil leaves

Method

Lightly brush the bread slices with olive oil. Drop sun-dried tomatoes in boiling water, drain and slice. Place remaining oil in a bowl. Add sliced tomatoes, olives, salt, pepper and herbs. Toss lightly and set aside for 10 to 15 minutes.

Preheat the oven to 350°F/180°C/Gas Mark 4. Divide the olive and tomato mixture equally between the bread slices. Cover with mozzarella cheese and bake in the oven until the cheese melts. Remove from the oven, garnish with basil and serve.

Serves } 8

Pizza Tartlets

Ingredients

For the tartlets

250 gm plain flour (sieved)

½ tsp salt

150 gm chilled butter, cut into ½ inch cubes

4 tbsp cold water

For the filling

1 tbsp butter

2 medium onions, finely chopped

1 large clove garlic, crushed

500 gm tomatoes, blanched and chopped

2 tsp (each) chopped basil and tomato purée

Salt, pepper and sugar to taste

To garnish

¼ cup (each) grated mozzarella cheese and sliced black olives

Method

For the tartlets

Sift the flour and salt in a bowl and rub in butter until mixture resembles breadcrumbs. Add water gradually and mix to a smooth dough. Wrap in a cling film and chill for 30 minutes. Roll out thinly on a floured surface and use to line twelve 2-inch tartlet moulds. Refrigerate for 30 minutes. Preheat the oven to 400°F/200°C/Gas Mark 6. Bake for 10 minutes. Remove from the oven and set aside to cool.

Makes 12-14 tartlets

For the filling

Melt butter in a pan; add onion and garlic. Cook gently until soft. Add tomato purée, chopped tomatoes, basil, salt, pepper and sugar. Simmer until almost all of the liquid has evaporated and mixture has thickened. Set aside to cool.

Place one heaped tablespoon of this mixture in each chilled pastry case and top with cheese and olives. Bake in a preheated oven for 12-15 minutes or until cheese has melted and pastry is slightly browned. Serve warm.

Traditional Pizza

Ingredients

2 tsp dry yeast

½ tsp sugar

1 cup warm water

2½ cups plain flour

1 tsp salt

9 tbsp olive oil

400 gm mozzarella cheese

Tomato-garlic Sauce (Page 56)

Method

Sprinkle the yeast and sugar over ¼ cup of lukewarm water. Let stand for 2-3 minutes, then stir until sugar is dissolved. Place in a warm place for 5-7 minutes, or until the yeast bubbles up and doubles in volume. Sift flour and salt in a large bowl. Make a well in the centre and pour in the yeast mixture and 3 tbsp of oil. Mix the dough with your fingers. When you can gather it into a rough ball, place the dough on a floured board and knead till smooth and elastic. Dust lightly with flour, place in a bowl, cover and place in a closed oven till double in size. When you want to use the dough, knead again on a floured board. Divide the dough into 4 parts.

Preheat the oven to 450°F/230°C/Gas Mark 8. Roll out one part into an 8-inch circle. Place on a large baking sheet. With your thumbs, crimp the edge of the circle until it forms a small rim. Brush the surface with a little oil. This prevents the dough from getting soggy.

Spread ½ cup of tomato-garlic sauce over the dough with the back of a spoon. Sprinkle ½ cup of mozzarella cheese and 1 tbsp oil and bake on the lowest shelf of the oven until the crust is lightly browned. Repeat this for the rest of the dough.

Makes 4 eight-inch pizzas

Pizza dough variation

1. Cornmeal dough: Substitute 1 cup maize flour for an equal amount of plain flour.
2. Herbed dough: Add 3 tbsp of freshly-chopped herbs while kneading the dough.
3. Wholewheat dough: Substitute 1 cup wholewheat flour for an equal amount of plain flour.
4. Spicy dough: Add 2 tbsp ground paprika and 1 tbsp black pepper to the flour while sieving with salt.

Alternative garnishes

1. Strips of green, red or yellow capsicums
2. Sliced olives, onions and capers
3. Sliced tomatoes and basil leaves
4. Sliced mushrooms
5. Boiled yellow corn kernels

Four Seasons Pizza

Pizza Quattro Stagione

Capsicums, red tomatoes, mushrooms and cheese form four triangles arranged over the pizza base and represent the colours and flavours of the four seasons: green capsicum for spring, red tomato for hot summer, earthy brown mushrooms for fall, and white cheese for winter snow.

Ingredients

Two 7-inch pizza bases

½ cup (each) thinly-sliced mushrooms, tomato and green capsicums

1 cup (each) grated mozzarella cheese and Tomato-garlic Sauce (recipe follows)

¼ cup olive oil

Salt, pepper and chilli flakes to taste

Method

Heat 2 tbsp of oil and sauté mushrooms until tender yet firm. Set aside. Repeat the same for the capsicums.

Make tomato-garlic sauce as per the recipe. Brush each pizza base with a little olive oil and spread ¼ cup sauce evenly on each one. Mark each pizza base in 4 equal sections. Arrange mushrooms on 1st section, capsicums on the 2nd section, cheese on the 3rd and little extra tomato-garlic sauce with tomato slices on the 4th one. Dribble remaining olive oil and bake at 350°F/180°C/ Gas Mark 4 for 15 minutes. Serve hot.

Serves } 4

Tomato-garlic Sauce

Ingredients

2 tbsp olive oil
2 medium onions, finely chopped
1 large carrot, grated
4 cloves garlic, minced
1 kg tomatoes, blanched and chopped
200 gm tomato purée
2 tbsp salt
½ tbsp pepper
½ tbsp (each) dried Italian seasoning and freshly-chopped basil
1 bay leaf

Method

In a saucepan heat the olive oil; sauté the onions, carrot and garlic. Cook until the vegetables are tender. Add the remaining ingredients and bring to a boil. Remove from heat, discard the bay leaf and set aside. At this point, you could purée half the mixture and blend it with the rest.

Makes 2 cups

Grilled Vegetable Pizza with Potato Crust

Ingredients

For the crust

2 cups grated raw potatoes (2-3 large potatoes)

1 medium onion, chopped

½ cup plain flour

1 tbsp olive oil

1 tsp salt

For the topping

1 medium zucchini, thinly sliced

1 medium red capsicum, thinly sliced

1 medium yellow capsicum, thinly sliced

1 small onion, thinly sliced

1 tbsp finely-chopped garlic

1 tbsp finely-chopped jalapeño chillies

2 tbsp olive oil

10 cherry tomatoes, quartered

8-10 fresh basil leaves

150 gm crumbled feta cheese

1 cup grated mozzarella cheese or pizza cheese

Method

For the crust

Preheat the oven to 400°F/200°C/Gas Mark 6.

Butter a 15 x 10-inch baking dish.

Place raw potatoes in a colander with salt and set aside for 10 minutes. Squeeze out excess water and place the potatoes in a bowl. Add onion and flour and mix well.

Pat potato mixture into the buttered baking dish and bake for 15 minutes. Brush with olive oil and bake for another 10 minutes. Place under the grill for 2-3 minutes until golden and crisp. Set aside.

For the topping

In a large bowl, combine the zucchini, capsicums, onion, garlic, jalapeño and 1 tbsp olive oil.

In a large frying pan, heat another tbsp of olive oil and sauté the vegetables until crisp and tender, stirring often. Remove from heat.

Spread feta cheese over the baked potato crust; top with cooked vegetables and tomatoes. Sprinkle with basil and mozzarella cheese.

Bake in the preheated oven for 5-7 minutes, or until the cheese has melted. Serve immediately.

Serves } 4-6

Polenta and Grilled Vegetables

with Roasted Red Pepper Sauce

Ingredients

1 cup uncooked instant polenta

2/3 cup grated Parmesan cheese

Salt and pepper to taste

Cooking spray or olive oil to grease the dish

2 cloves garlic, chopped

2 tbsp fresh thyme or oregano

or

1 tbsp dried oregano

1/4 cup fresh lemon juice

1 tbsp olive oil

500 gm assorted vegetables (such as asparagus, onions, cherry tomatoes, zucchini, cut into lengths)

For the sauce

3 medium red capsicums, roasted and peeled

1/3 cup Vegetable Stock (Page 245)

1 clove garlic, chopped

3 tbsp chopped parsley, chives or basil

1 tbsp balsamic vinegar

Salt to taste

To garnish

Sprigs of parsley and basil and a few stalks of chives

Method

Bring 3 cups of water to boil in a medium pan. Add polenta in a thin stream, stirring continuously. Lower the heat and cook, stirring continuously for 3-5 minutes or until thick. Add one-third cup Parmesan cheese and season with salt and pepper.

Coat a 9-inch pie dish with cooking spray or olive oil. Transfer the polenta to the pie dish, smooth the top and set aside.

Mix garlic, thyme, lemon juice, salt, pepper and oil in a bowl. Toss the vegetables in this dressing and spread on a baking sheet. Place under the grill for 7-8 minutes or until vegetables are slightly charred. Remove and set aside.

For the sauce

Combine all the ingredients for the sauce in a blender jar and process until smooth. Transfer to a saucepan and warm slightly.

Sprinkle remaining one-third cup Parmesan on the polenta and place under the grill until golden brown for 2-3 minutes. Cut into 8 triangles.

Divide vegetables amongst 8 individual plates, arranging them neatly. Place one triangle of polenta on each plate and drizzle the sauce over the vegetables. Garnish with herbs and serve.

Serves } 6-8

Note: If you wish to serve polenta in one large dish, place the vegetables in the centre of a large plate, drizzle the sauce over and arrange polenta wedges all around. Garnish with parsley, basil and chives. Serve hot.

Broccoli Pizza Pie

Ingredients

For the crust

3 large potatoes, boiled and peeled

1/4 cup cream cheese

2 cups broccoli florets, boiled

1/2 cup grated pizza cheese

2 tsp crushed garlic

2 tsp chopped basil

3/4 tsp oregano

3/4 tsp parsley

1/2 cup milk

1/2 cup cream

1 tbsp breadcrumbs

Salt, pepper and mustard to taste

To garnish

Sprig of parsley and carrot curls

To serve

Pizza sauce

Method

For the crust

Mash the potatoes – you should get 1 1/3 cups. Mix together the potatoes and cream cheese until smooth. Spoon the mixture into a 9-inch pie dish and spread over the bottom and sides to form a crust. Arrange broccoli on the potato crust. Sprinkle cheese, garlic and herbs. In another small bowl, mix milk and cream. Add salt, pepper and mustard. Pour this over the cheese. Sprinkle with breadcrumbs and bake in an oven preheated to 350°F/180°C/Gas Mark 4 for 30-35 minutes. Remove from the oven, garnish with carrot curls and parsley and serve with pizza sauce.

Serves } 6

Italian Potato Pie

Ingredients

For the crust

600 gm potatoes, boiled and mashed

3 tbsp softened butter

1/3 cup (each) Sour Cream (Page 245) and grated Parmesan cheese

½ cup finely-chopped spring onions

200 gm sliced mozzarella cheese

2 medium tomatoes, blanched and sliced

1 tsp (each) dried basil and oregano

3 tbsp melted butter

Salt and pepper to taste

Method

Mix softened butter with the mashed potatoes while they are still hot. Add sour cream, spring onions, salt and pepper. Lightly grease and dust an 8" pie dish. Spread the potato mixture evenly. Arrange ½ of the mozzarella cheese on the potatoes. Top with tomatoes. Sprinkle basil and oregano. Top with remaining mozzarella, Parmesan cheese and melted butter. Bake at 350°F/180°C/Gas Mark 4 for 20-25 minutes, or until cheese melts. Cool slightly before cutting.

Serves } 6

Chilli Risotto with Mushroom and Balsamic Reduction

Ingredients

For the risotto

1 tbsp butter

1 tbsp olive oil

½ cup finely-chopped onion

1 tbsp crushed garlic

1 cup arborio or carnaroli risotto rice

3-3½ cups Vegetable Stock (Page 245)

½ cup finely-chopped red and yellow capsicums

2 tbsp finely-chopped jalapeño chillies

Salt and pepper to taste

½ cup cream

¼ cup grated Parmesan cheese

For the potato base

250 gm potatoes, peeled and thinly sliced

2 tbsp olive oil

For the balsamic reduction

2 tbsp olive oil

1 cup finely-chopped mushrooms

1 tsp dried oregano

½ glass red wine (60 ml)

½ cup Vegetable Stock (Page 245)

½ cup cream

2 tbsp balsamic vinegar

Salt and pepper to taste

To garnish

2-3 fried spaghetti sticks and chives

Method

Melt butter and olive oil in a heavy saucepan; add onion and garlic and sauté until translucent. Add rice and mix well. Heat the stock, and add gradually to the rice, stirring continuously, making sure that the stock is absorbed completely before each addition. Add capsicums and jalapeño chillies and cook until soft. Season with salt and pepper and finally add the cream and Parmesan cheese.

For the balsamic reduction

Heat the olive oil in a small pan and add mushrooms, oregano and wine. Simmer gently until the liquid is reduced by half. Add the stock and simmer gently until thick. Add balsamic vinegar and cream and cook over a low heat for a few minutes. Add salt and pepper, take off heat and set aside.

Grease a 4-cup capacity ovenproof mould with olive oil and arrange the sliced potatoes overlapping each other. Sprinkle with salt and bake at 350°F/180°C/Gas Mark 4 for 8-10 minutes. Remove the dish from the oven and ladle the prepared risotto on top, pressing down lightly. Cover and bake for 5 minutes. In a serving dish, pour the balsamic reduction and invert the risotto mould on it. Garnish with fried spaghetti and chives.

Serves } 6

Tortellini

Pasta Filled with Ricotta and Spinach

Ingredients

For the dough

150 gm plain flour, sieved

1 egg

1 egg white

1 tbsp olive oil

1 tsp salt

For the filling

200 gm Ricotta Cheese (Page 52)

100 gm mozzarella cheese

100 gm Parmesan cheese

½ cup chopped and washed spinach

2 tbsp fresh cream

1 tbsp freshly-chopped parsley and basil

½ tsp nutmeg

½ tsp salt

½ tsp pepper

To serve

2 cups Cheese Sauce (Page 74)

Melted butter and Parmesan cheese

Method

For the filling

Mix the cheeses, spinach, herbs, cream, salt, pepper and nutmeg in a large bowl until thoroughly combined. Set aside.

For the tortellini

Mix all the ingredients together and make a pliable dough. Break off half of the dough and roll it in the machine or by hand, several times to make smooth sheets. Roll out until paper thin. Cut into 2-inch rounds with a cookie cutter.

Place 1 tsp of the cheese mixture in the centre of each round. Moisten the edges. Fold the circles in half and press firmly together. Shape into little rings by stretching the tips of each half-circle slightly and wrapping the ring around your index finger. Gently press the tips together. Immerse the tortellini in boiling water a few at a time. Stir with a wooden spoon to make sure they don't stick together. Boil for 8 minutes or until tender. Drain through a large sieve. Serve hot with butter, Parmesan and cheese sauce.

Makes approximately 20 tortellini

Note: Tortellini is best if cooked at once.

Pasta Aglio e Olio

Ingredients

200 grams pasta of your choice

3 tablespoons olive oil

6 cloves garlic, crushed

1 tablespoon basil, chopped

Salt, black pepper powder and chilli flakes to taste

Method

Cook the pasta in boiling salted water, until *al dente* (cooked, but firm to the bite). Drain and place under running cold water. Drain again. In a large frying pan, heat olive oil; add garlic, basil and chilli flakes and fry for two minutes on medium heat. Add drained pasta, salt and pepper. Serve hot pasta by itself or accompanied by a pasta sauce.

Serves } 4

Penne Arrabiata

Ingredients

For the pasta

225 gm penne (fluted pasta), boiled and drained

2 tbsp olive oil

2 tbsp freshly-chopped parsley, basil and chives

2-3 cloves garlic, crushed (optional)

A pinch of chilli flakes

Salt to taste

For the arrabiata sauce

4-5 tomatoes, blanched and chopped

1 medium onion, finely chopped

1 tbsp finely-chopped basil

1 tbsp finely-chopped parsley

3-4 cloves garlic, crushed

1-2 tsp chilli flakes

½ tsp salt

½ tsp pepper

1 tbsp olive oil

4-5 tbsp fresh cream

To serve

Freshly-grated Parmesan and truffle oil

Method

For the pasta

Heat oil in a frying pan; add garlic, herbs and chilli flakes. Fry for half a minute and add boiled pasta and salt. Toss gently to mix. Remove from the heat and set aside.

For the arrabiata sauce

Heat the oil in a saucepan and fry garlic and onion until soft. Add tomatoes, salt, pepper and chilli flakes. Bring to a boil and add herbs. Just before serving, gently add the cream and mix well. Serve hot with tossed pasta.

Makes 1½ cups

How to serve

Reheat the pasta on a low heat, turn out onto an individual pasta dish and pour the sauce over. Serve grated cheese and truffle oil on the side.

Serves } 4

Olive & Sun-dried Tomato Crostini
(recipe on page 53)

Chilli Risotto with Mushroom and Balsamic Reduction
(recipe on page 61)

Ravioli

Stuffed Pasta Pockets

Ingredients

For the dough

200 gm plain flour

1 egg

1 egg white

¾ tbsp oil

1 tsp salt

3 tbsp water

For eggless dough

2 cups plain flour

½ cup warm water

1 tbsp oil

½ tsp baking powder

½ tsp salt

For the filling

200 gm spinach leaves

5-6 tbsp Parmesan cheese

200 gm Ricotta Cheese (Page 52)

1 tbsp plain flour

2 tbsp grated onion

Salt, pepper and nutmeg to taste

To serve

2 tbsp melted butter

1½ cups pasta sauce such as Cheese Sauce (Page 74) or Marinara Sauce (Page 76)

Freshly-grated Parmesan cheese

Method

For the dough

Pour the flour into a large mixing bowl; make a well in the centre, add the egg and egg white, oil and salt. Mix together with a fork, until the dough comes together in a rough ball. Moisten any remaining dry bits with drops of water and press into the ball. Cover with a damp cloth and rest the dough for half an hour.

Make the eggless pasta dough in the same way but without adding the eggs. Knead for 10-15 minutes, cover and rest the dough for 20 minutes.

To make pasta with a machine

Use one-third of the dough at a time. Dust the dough lightly with flour and roll it 4 to 5 times through the rollers at the widest setting. When the dough is smooth and elastic, roll it out, setting the machine at the second notch with the rollers closer together. Roll a very thin sheet of pasta.

Pasta and Roasted Vegetables in Spicy Sauce (recipe on page 69)

Broccoli Pizza Pie (recipe on page 59)

To make pasta by hand

Divide the dough into half. Place 1 ball on a floured surface and flatten it with your hand into a 1-inch thick oblong. Dust the top lightly with flour and using a very heavy rolling pin roll out the dough with up and down movements until it is paper-thin. If the dough sticks, lift carefully and sprinkle more flour under it. Cut into long thin sheets, cut again into two and set aside. Cover the rolled pasta to avoid drying. Roll out all the pasta in the same way.

For the filling

Wash, cook and grind the spinach to a paste. In a large bowl, mix together the spinach paste, ricotta and Parmesan cheeses, flour, onion, salt, pepper and nutmeg. Set aside.

To prepare the stuffed pasta

Place the rolled out sheet on a working surface. Place mounds of 1 tbsp of cheese and spinach mixture 2 inches apart across and down the pasta sheet. Dip your index finger into a bowl of water and make vertical and horizontal lines in a chessboard pattern on the pasta sheet, between the mounds of filling. Carefully cover with another sheet of rolled pasta. Press down firmly around the filling and along the wetted lines. With a ravioli cutter or pastry wheel cut the pasta into squares. Separate the pieces of ravioli, cover with a sheet of paper and set aside.

Alternatively, if you have a ravioli machine, press pasta sheet on the tray, place the filling on the pasta and press another sheet over. Roll with the rolling pin provided. Separate the ravioli squares and set aside.

Cook ravioli a few pieces at a time in boiling salted water for 7-8 minutes. Stir gently with a wooden spoon to keep them from sticking together. Drain.

To serve

Toss ravioli in melted butter and either pour the heated sauce over on individual portions or serve the sauce separately on the side. Sprinkle freshly-grated Parmesan on top.

Serves } 6

Pasta with Pink Sauce

Ingredients

1 tbsp olive oil

2-3 cloves garlic, crushed

1 tsp dried mixed herbs

200 gm pasta of your choice, boiled

1 tbsp butter

1 medium onion, finely chopped

1 tbsp plain flour

3-4 medium tomatoes, blanched and chopped

Salt, pepper and chilli flakes to taste

¾ cup milk + ¼ cup cream

1 tbsp tomato purée

½ cup grated Cheddar cheese

To garnish

Fresh basil leaves and grated Cheddar or mozzarella cheese

Method

In a wide pan, heat the olive oil; add garlic and sauté for 1 minute. Add herbs, pasta and ½ tsp salt and set aside. In another heavy saucepan, melt the butter; add onion and cook until soft. Add the flour and cook for 1 minute longer. Add the tomatoes, salt, pepper and chilli flakes and mix well. Remove from heat and gradually add the milk and cream mixture, making sure no lumps are formed. Return to heat and boil for 2-3 minutes. Stir in the tomato purée and cheese and set aside.

Just before serving, reheat the sauce, add the flavoured pasta and mix gently. Place the pan on heat and cook until heated through. Turn out onto a serving dish, garnish with basil and serve hot with additional grated cheese on top.

Serves } 4

Pasta Stuffed with Cottage Cheese

Ingredients

200 gm abissina rigate (shell-shaped) pasta, boiled

200 gm Ricotta (Page 52) or cottage cheese

¼ cup finely-chopped onion

¼ cup finely-chopped tomato

¼ cup finely-chopped red capsicum

1 tbsp finely-chopped basil

Salt and pepper to taste

For the sauce

1 tbsp butter

1 tbsp plain flour

½ cup milk

½ cup cream

¼ cup grated Parmesan cheese

Salt, pepper and nutmeg to taste

Flavouring for the cheese sauce (choose any one):

1. A red or yellow capsicum, roasted and puréed
2. 100 gm mushrooms, finely chopped and sautéed
3. ½ cup tomato purée with 1 tbsp chopped basil
4. ¼ cup sun-dried tomatoes, soaked and puréed
5. ¼ cup Pesto Sauce (Page 75) mixed with ¼ cup pasta water

To garnish

Grated Cheddar or mozzarella cheese

Method

In a medium bowl, mix together ricotta or cottage cheese, onion, tomato, red capsicum, basil, salt and pepper. Stuff pasta shells with this mixture and set aside.

For the sauce

Melt butter in a thick saucepan; add the flour and cook for 2 minutes. Remove from heat and add the milk and stir well. Return to the stove and add the cream, Parmesan, salt, pepper and nutmeg. Bring to a boil, lower heat and add the chosen flavouring. Place the stuffed pasta on a greased baking dish and pour the sauce over. Garnish with grated cheese and bake at 350°F/180°C/Gas Mark 4 for 10-12 minutes.

Serves } 6

Pasta and Roasted Vegetables in Spicy Sauce

Ingredients

250 gm pasta, cooked and tossed with olive oil

500 gm roasted vegetables of your choice

Butter to grease the dish

For the sauce

1 cup milk

2 tbsp plain flour

1 tbsp butter

1 medium onion, finely chopped

2-3 cloves crushed garlic

2 large tomatoes, blanched and chopped

500 gm roasted red capsicum, puréed

2 tbsp (each) freshly-chopped basil and parsley

Salt, pepper and red chilli flakes to taste

To serve

Parmesan cheese

Method

For the sauce

Mix milk and flour in a saucepan and boil until thickened. Set aside. In another pan melt butter and cook onion and garlic until slightly soft. Add the tomatoes, puréed capsicum, parsley and basil. Add this mixture to thickened milk and flour. Season the sauce with salt, pepper and chilli flakes. Mix well.

For the pasta

Mix pasta with grilled vegetables and season with salt and pepper. Grease baking dish with butter. Line it with the pasta-vegetable mixture and even out the surface. Pour prepared sauce over evenly. Sprinkle Parmesan cheese and bake in an oven at 325°F/170°C/Gas Mark 3 for 10-15 minutes. Serve hot.

Serves } 6

Broccoli Lasagna

Ingredients

200 gm lasagna sheets, boiled

½ cup red capsicum, chopped

½ cup green capsicum, chopped

½ cup onion, chopped

1 clove garlic, minced

3 tbsp basil, chopped

350 gm broccoli, separated into florets

2 cups cottage cheese, crumbled

1½ cups Marinara Sauce (Page 76)

1½ cups Cheese Sauce (Page 74)

100 gm mozzarella cheese, grated

1 tbsp olive oil

1 tsp butter

Salt and pepper to taste

Method

Grease a 10 in x 6 in rectangular baking dish with butter. Steam the broccoli and set aside. In a frying pan, heat oil and sauté the onion and garlic. Add capsicums and cook for 5-7 minutes. Add broccoli, basil, salt and pepper. Take off heat and add crumbled cottage cheese. Mix together both the sauces.

Preheat the oven to 350°F/180°C/Gas Mark 4. In the baking dish spread one-third of the sauce mixture and place the lasagna sheets over the sauce. Spread the broccoli-capsicum mixture over it with half the remaining sauce mixture and one-third of the grated cheese. Continue until you get 3 layers. The top layer should be sauce and cheese. Bake in the preheated oven for 10-15 minutes.

Serves } 4

Mushroom and Corn Lasagna

Ingredients

200 gm lasagna noodles, boiled

½ cup chopped onion

3-4 cloves garlic, minced

3 tbsp basil and parsley, chopped

½ cup yellow corn kernels, boiled

2 packets mushrooms, washed and sliced

2 cups cottage cheese, crumbled

1½ cups Marinara Sauce (Page 76)

1½ cups Cheese Sauce (Page 74)

100 gm mozzarella cheese, grated

1 tbsp olive oil

1 tsp butter

Salt and pepper to taste

Method

Grease a 10 in×6 in rectangular baking dish with butter. In a frying pan, heat oil and sauté the onion and garlic. Add mushrooms and cook till soft. Add corn, herbs, salt and pepper. Take off heat and add crumbled cottage cheese. Mix together both the sauces.

Preheat the oven to 350°F/180°C/Gas Mark 4.

In the baking dish spread one-third of the sauce mixture and place the lasagna noodles over the sauce. Spread the mushroom-corn mixture over it with half the remaining sauce mixture and one-third of the grated cheese. Continue until you get 3 layers. The top layer should be sauce and cheese. Bake in the preheated oven for 10-15 minutes.

Serves } 4

Pesto and Herb Dip

Ingredients

250 gm cream cheese

1 tbsp Pesto Sauce (Page 75)

1 tbsp finely chopped chives

¼ cup finely chopped almonds

To serve

Freshly-cut vegetable sticks, bread sticks or crackers

Method

Place cheese and pesto sauce in food processor and process until smooth. Add chives and mix well. Spoon this mixture into a 4-inch round mould and freeze for 2-3 hours. Turn out on a serving plate and coat with almonds. Serve with vegetable sticks, bread sticks or crackers.

Serves } 4-6

Note: For the crudités, here are some fresh raw vegetables you could use:

1. *Broccoli or cauliflower florets*
2. *Carrot strips*
3. *Celery strips*
4. *Mushroom quarters*
5. *Courgette (zucchini) fingers*

Ricotta Cheese and Red Pepper Dip

Ingredients

3 medium red capsicums, roasted and skin removed

2 stems spring onions, coarsely chopped

1 tsp ready mustard

1 tsp finely-chopped garlic

200 gm Ricotta Cheese (Page 52), crumbled

2 tbsp olive oil

1 tbsp wine vinegar

Salt, pepper and Tabasco sauce to taste

To serve

Assorted crackers and crudités

Method

Place capsicums, spring onions and garlic in a food processor and process until the mixture is smooth. Add the cheese and mustard and process till well-blended. With the motor running, dribble the oil in and blend well. Add vinegar and blend again. Scrape the mixture into a serving bowl. Add Tabasco, salt and pepper to taste. Chill for 1-2 hours. Serve with crackers or crudités.

Serves } 8

Tomato Basil Sauce

Ingredients

2 tbsp corn or olive oil

2 to 3 onions, finely chopped

50 gm tomatoes, blanched and coarsely chopped

2 tbsp tomato paste

1 tsp sugar

2 tsp each salt and freshly-ground pepper

50 gm fresh basil leaves

Method

In a saucepan, heat oil; add onions and cook over medium heat until soft. Add tomatoes, tomato paste, basil, sugar, salt and pepper. Reduce heat, cover and cook for 30 minutes, stirring occasionally. Press through a sieve into a bowl, adjust seasoning and serve hot with fresh pasta.

Cheese Sauce

Ingredients

2 tbsp butter

2 tbsp plain flour

1 cup milk

1 cup cream

2 tbsp Parmesan cheese

A dash of nutmeg

Salt, pepper and mustard to taste

Method

Melt butter in a pan; add the flour and stir for 3-4 minutes. Take the pan off the heat and stir in milk gradually, mixing well to make sure that no lumps are formed. Place the pan on heat again, add the seasoning, bring to a boil and remove from heat. Stir in the cream and cheese. Serve hot with pasta.

Makes 2 cups

Pesto Sauce

Ingredients

1 tbsp finely chopped garlic

1½ cups fresh basil leaves stripped from their stems

1 tsp salt

2 tsp black pepper

5 tsp chopped and toasted walnuts or pine nuts

¾ cup olive oil

50 gm freshly grated Parmesan cheese.

Method

In a blender, combine basil, salt, pepper, garlic, walnuts and oil. Blend at high speed until smooth. The sauce should be thin enough to run off a spatula easily. Transfer the sauce to a bowl and stir in the grated cheese. Serve the pesto thoroughly mixed into hot, drained pasta, tossed with soft butter, or use as a dip or sandwich spread.

Serves } 4

Note: The pesto is often thinned further by adding to it 1-2 tbsp of the hot pasta water before mixing it with the pasta.

Marinara Sauce

Ingredients

2 tbsp olive oil

2 medium onions, finely chopped

1 large carrot, grated

1 large green capsicum, finely chopped

4 cloves garlic, minced

1 kg tomatoes, blanched and chopped

1 cup tomato purée

2 tbsp salt

½ tbsp pepper

1 tbsp mixed dried herbs

1 bay leaf

Method

In a saucepan, heat olive oil and sauté the onions, carrot, capsicum and garlic. Cook until the vegetables are tender. Add the remaining ingredients and bring to a boil. Remove from heat. At this point, you could purée half the sauce and mix with the rest.

Serve hot with the pasta.

Makes 3 cups

Sun-dried Tomato Pesto

Ingredients

100 gm sun-dried tomatoes, dropped in hot water for 20 minutes

2 cloves garlic

¾ cup blanched almonds

3 tbsp parsley

3 tbsp basil

½ cup olive oil

¾ cup grated Parmesan cheese

1 tsp balsamic vinegar

Grated rind of 1 lemon

Salt and pepper to taste

Method

Place lemon rind, garlic, tomatoes, almonds, parsley and basil in a food processor and blend until smooth. With the motor running, slowly pour in the oil. Blend till all the oil is incorporated. Add the vinegar and blend again. Transfer the mixture to a bowl and add the Parmesan cheese, salt and pepper. Store the spread in an airtight jar in the refrigerator. Use as a spread on crusty bread or dilute with fresh cream and use as sauce for pasta.

Makes 2 cups

Mediterranean

Exotic names like Muttabal, Tzatziki, Escalibada, Gazpacho and Moussaka entice you into the wonderful world of Mediterranean cuisine! Salads garnished with heart-healthy olive oil, platters of feta cheese and bowls of aromatic soup, including the intriguing Orange Lentil Soup, Spicy Eggplant Salad, Smoked Cottage Cheese and Red Pepper Shots, Vegetable Tajine with Couscous and the flavourful Spanish Tapas...

Roasted Red Pepper and Pine Nut Soup

Ingredients

4 medium red capsicums

¼ cup oil

4 medium tomatoes

1 tsp dried mixed herbs

2 cloves garlic, chopped

1 medium onion, chopped

1 medium leek, sliced

2 medium carrots, chopped

2 tbsp toasted and chopped pine nuts

4 cups water or thin Vegetable Stock (Page 245)

1 tsp sweet chilli sauce

Salt and pepper to taste

To garnish

Fresh herbs and Sour Cream (Page 245)

Method

Cut the capsicums into quarters. Brush each piece with a little oil and grill until the skin blackens slightly. Leave to cool and remove the skin. Cut the tomatoes and scoop out the seeds.

In a large pan, heat the oil and add the herbs and garlic. Stir over a low heat for 1 minute. Add the onion and leek and cook for 3 minutes until golden. Add tomatoes, capsicums, carrots, pine nuts and water or stock. Bring to a boil and simmer for 20 minutes. Remove from the heat and set aside to cool.

Process the soup in a blender and pass it through a sieve. Return to heat; add the chilli sauce and season with salt and pepper. Garnish with herbs and sour cream. Serve hot.

Serves | 4–6

Country Soup

Soupa Horiátiki

Ingredients

2 medium potatoes, diced

2 medium carrots, diced

2 medium courgettes, diced

2-3 medium tomatoes, sliced

2 medium leeks, sliced

½ cup boiled cannellini (beans)

2 tbsp olive oil

2 medium onions, diced

1 large clove garlic, sliced

4 cups Vegetable Stock (Page 245)

Salt, pepper and lemon juice to taste

To serve
Crusty bread

Method

Heat oil in a saucepan; sauté onion and garlic until transparent. Add the vegetables, cannellini beans, stock, salt and pepper. Bring to a boil and simmer until vegetables are soft. Stir in lemon juice to taste and serve the soup hot with crusty bread.

Serves } 8

Tomato Soup with Artichoke, Beans and Roasted Peppers

Ingredients

½ cup white beans, soaked overnight and boiled

4 cups water

2 stock cubes

2 tbsp Worcestershire sauce

1 tsp Tabasco sauce

1 tbsp (each) balsamic vinegar and chopped garlic

1 cup finely-chopped onion

1 stick celery, finely chopped

3 medium roasted red capsicums, peeled and chopped

750 gm tomatoes, blanched and chopped

1 tin (450gm) artichoke hearts, chopped

1 tbsp (each) sugar, basil, oregano and thyme

Salt and pepper to taste

Method

Place beans with the water in which they were boiled on the stove. Add 4 cups of water, stock cube, Worcestershire sauce, Tabasco, balsamic vinegar, onion, celery and garlic. Simmer this for 20 minutes. Add capsicums and the remaining ingredients. Simmer for 5-10 minutes more.

Serves } 8

Mediterranean Dip Platter
(recipe on page 105)

Shorabat Adas

Orange Lentil Soup

Ingredients

2 tbsp olive oil

1 medium onion, coarsely chopped

1 large clove garlic, crushed

2 cups orange lentils, washed and rinsed

6 cups Vegetable Stock (Page 245)

1 tsp (each) cumin powder and salt

½ tsp pepper powder

To garnish

Lemon wedges, whole olives and red radishes

To serve

Wholewheat toast brushed with olive oil

Method

Heat the oil in a pressure cooker pan over medium heat. Add the onion and garlic; sauté until soft. Add the lentils and stir to coat in oil. Add the stock, close the lid and cook for 3 whistles. Set aside to cool.

Transfer the soup to a blender in batches and purée. Return the soup to a pan. Add salt, cumin and pepper. Mix well. Bring to a boil and then simmer the soup for 10-15 minutes.

Ladle the soup into bowls, garnish with lemon wedges, olives and radishes on a toothpick placed across the bowl. Serve with wholewheat toast.

Serves } 8

Green Gazpacho

Ingredients

2 cups chopped lettuce leaves

2 cups chopped spinach leaves

3 spring onion stems, finely chopped

1 medium cucumber, peeled and chopped

2 cloves garlic, chopped

1 tbsp lemon juice

1 tbsp chopped parsley

½ cup sour cream

2 cups Vegetable Stock (Page 245)

1 tsp finely-chopped mint leaves

½ tsp salt

½ tsp pepper

To garnish

Sour Cream (Page 245) and bread croutons

Method

Combine lettuce, spinach, spring onion stems, cucumber, garlic, lemon juice and parsley in a blender and purée till smooth. Gradually add sour cream, stock, mint, salt and pepper. Blend once again until smooth.

Transfer to a bowl and chill until ready to serve.

Ladle the soup into individual bowls and garnish with sour cream and croutons.

Serves } 4-6

Gazpacho Mould

Ingredients

For the soup

2 tsp unflavoured gelatine

¼ cup Vegetable Stock (Page 245)

1 small onion, chopped

2 cloves garlic

3 tbsp olive oil

2 tbsp red wine vinegar

2 cups tomato juice

¼ cup chopped cucumber

¼ cup chopped red capsicum

Salt and pepper to taste

Tabasco, Worcestershire sauce and lemon juice to taste

To garnish

¼ cup finely-chopped cucumber

¼ cup finely-chopped green capsicum

1 stick celery, finely chopped

2-3 tbsp finely-chopped chives

To serve

Toasted bread

Method

Dissolve the gelatine in the vegetable stock. Purée the next four ingredients in a blender, add the tomato juice, cucumber, capsicum and gelatine mixture and blend to mix well. Season well with salt, pepper, Tabasco, Worcestershire and lemon juice to taste.

Grease a 5-cup capacity mould with a little oil. Sprinkle all the ingredients for the garnish on the base of the mould. Pour the puréed mixture over the vegetables in the mould. Cover and chill for 1 hour or until set. Unmould onto a serving plate and serve with toasted bread.

Serves } 6-8

Greek Country Salad

Saláta Horiátiki

Ingredients

1 large head iceberg lettuce

3-4 tomatoes, cut into wedges

2 medium cucumbers, peeled and thinly sliced

1 medium onion, thinly sliced

1 medium red capsicum, thinly sliced

200 gm feta cheese, cubed

½ cup sliced black olives

For the dressing

3-4 tbsp olive oil

2-3 tbsp vinegar

½ tsp salt

½ tsp pepper

½ tsp basil

½ tsp mint

½ tsp thyme

½ tsp oregano

Note: This salad is an excellent filling for a pita sandwich.

Method

Wash and prepare all the vegetables as instructed. Place in a bowl along with the olives, cover with cling film and chill.

For the dressing, combine all the ingredients in a small bottle, close tightly and shake gently. Pour into a small bowl and gently toss feta cheese in the dressing. Set aside for half an hour. Just before serving, pour the dressing over the vegetables and toss gently.

Serves } 6

Chickpea, Broccoli and Roasted Pepper Salad

Ingredients

150 gm chickpeas, soaked overnight and boiled

2 medium red capsicums, roasted, peeled and cubed

200 gm broccoli, cut into florets and blanched

¼ cup sliced black or green olives

2-3 spring onion stems, sliced

For the dressing

6 tbsp olive oil

1 tsp balsamic vinegar

1 tbsp finely-chopped parsley

1 tbsp finely-chopped oregano

1 tbsp finely-chopped garlic

Salt, pepper and chilli flakes to taste

Method

Combine all the salad ingredients in a bowl and place in a refrigerator to chill.

Mix all the ingredients for the dressing in a jar and shake to mix well. Pour the dressing over the prepared salad and toss gently. Serve chilled.

Serves } 4

Zaalouk

Spicy Eggplant Salad

Ingredients

700 gm eggplant, peeled and cubed

5 cloves garlic, crushed

3-4 large tomatoes, peeled and chopped

4 tbsp extra virgin olive oil

2 tbsp wine vinegar

1 tsp (each) harissa, chilli flakes and ground cumin

½ cup freshly-chopped parsley

Salt and sugar to taste

To garnish
Lettuce leaves and toasted pine nuts

To serve
Pita bread

Method

Toss eggplant with 1 tbsp olive oil and ½ tsp salt; place in a tray under a grill. Cook until slightly charred.

In a small bowl mix together remaining olive oil, garlic, vinegar, harissa, chilli flakes, cumin, salt and sugar. Toss eggplant with this mixture and add the tomatoes and parsley.

Line a shallow bowl with lettuce leaves and transfer the salad gently to the centre of the serving dish. Garnish with pine nuts and serve with warm pita bread.

Serves } 6

Lebanese Salad

Ingredients

¼ cup (each) sun-dried tomatoes and olives

½ cup feta cheese, cubed

2-3 stems sliced spring onions

1 small (each) red and yellow capsicum, blanched and cubed

2 tbsp (each) finely-chopped parsley, basil, olive oil and pine nuts

2-3 cloves garlic, crushed

½ tsp (each) chilli flakes, salt and pepper

1 tsp balsamic vinegar

To garnish

A bunch of basil leaves

Method

Soak sun-dried tomatoes in hot water for 15-20 minutes. Drain and slice them thinly. Mix all the ingredients together in a bowl and toss them gently. Chill until ready to serve.

Serves } 6

Yogurt and Cucumber Salad

Ingredients

2-3 medium cucumbers, peeled and thinly sliced

3 cups thick yogurt

3 cloves garlic, crushed with a little salt

10-12 fresh mint leaves, coarsely chopped

1 tbsp lemon juice

Salt to taste

Method

Mix all the ingredients together in a serving bowl and chill.

Serves } 4-6

Fattoush

Bread Salad

Ingredients

1 loaf pita bread

2 firm tomatoes, chopped

1 cup lettuce leaves, cut into square pieces

1 cucumber, chopped

2 onions, finely chopped

1 bunch parsley, finely chopped

2 tbsp fresh mint, finely chopped

3 tbsp fresh coriander, finely chopped

2 cloves garlic, crushed

6 tbsp olive oil

1 tsp dry pomegranate seeds, powdered

Juice of 2 lemons

Salt and pepper to taste

To garnish

A handful of toasted pine nuts

Method

Open out the pita loaf and toast it crisp and brown, then crush it with your hands to break it into little pieces. Put these pieces in a bowl, moisten with little lemon juice and set aside.

Mix all the other ingredients in a large salad bowl and refrigerate until ready to use.

Just before serving mix toasted bread pieces, garnish with nuts and serve.

Serves } 4–6

Cottage Cheese Shawerma

Ingredients

500 gm cottage cheese, cut into thin strips

2 tbsp olive oil

1 cup chopped tomatoes

2-3 tbsp chopped parsley or coriander

2 medium onions, sliced

6 thin loaves pita bread

Marinade

¼ cup olive oil

3 tbsp brown vinegar

2 medium onions, chopped

¼ cup finely-chopped parsley or coriander

1 tbsp fresh thyme

2 tbsp oregano

3-4 dried red chillies

3-4 cloves garlic

1 tbsp ginger

½ tsp pepper

3 tbsp tahina paste

3 tbsp thick yogurt

½ tsp salt

2 tbsp lemon juice

To serve

Sliced lemons, pickled vegetables, garlic cream, and taratour sauce (recipes follow)

Method

Grind all the ingredients for the marinade to a paste. Marinate cottage cheese in the paste for 1 hour. Heat 2 tbsp of olive oil; cook the marinated cottage cheese pieces until golden brown. If the mixture feels dry, add a little water to prevent sticking. Just before removing from heat, move the cottage cheese to the edges of the pan. Place a live piece of coal with a drop of oil on it in the centre. Cover the pan tightly for 2 minutes. Remove the cover and add tomatoes, parsley or coriander and sliced onions. Cook for 3-4 minutes.

Toast each pita bread loaf lightly over heat; splash some of the garlic cream all over and spoon some of the cottage cheese mixture at one end.

Roll up and serve immediately along with pickled vegetables, garlic cream, taratour sauce and sliced lemon.

Serves } 4-6

Pickled Vegetables

Mix together 1 thinly-sliced cucumber, 1 sliced tomato, 1 thinly-sliced carrot, 1 tbsp each of lemon juice and vinegar, 2 crushed cloves of garlic, 2 tbsp olive oil, salt and pepper to taste. Set aside for 4-6 hours.

Garlic Cream

Blend peeled cloves of 2 whole bulbs of garlic, ½ cup lemon juice and ½ tbsp salt until smooth. With the motor running, slowly add 1½ cups olive oil in a thin stream. Blend till the mixture reaches the consistency of thick mayonnaise.

Taratour Sauce

Mix together 2 tbsp tahina paste, 1 tsp crushed garlic, 1 tbsp lemon juice, ½ cup yogurt and salt to taste. Chill.

Greek-style Spinach Pastry

Ingredients

12-14 wonton wrappers or squares of phyllo pastry

2 cups spinach leaves

1 tbsp butter

1 tbsp plain flour

Salt, pepper and nutmeg to taste

1 cup crumbled feta cheese

¼ cup finely-chopped walnuts or pine nuts

Melted butter to brush the pastry

Method

Boil and purée the spinach leaves. In a small pan, melt 1 tbsp butter; add plain flour and cook for 1 minute. Add puréed spinach, salt, pepper and nutmeg. Cook until all the water has dried up. Remove and set aside to cool. Mix in the crumbled feta cheese and nuts.

Place each wonton wrapper/phyllo pastry square on a board and brush lightly with melted butter. Spoon 1 tbsp of spinach mixture in the centre. Lift up one corner of the wrapper and roll up towards the opposite corner. Press lightly to seal. Twist the roll into a half-moon shape.

Place all the pastries on a baking sheet. Brush with melted butter and bake in a hot oven at 375° F/190°C/Gas Mark 5 for 15-20 minutes or until golden brown. Serve hot.

Makes 12-14 pastries

Greek Roll-ups

Ingredients

6 sheets phyllo pastry or puff pastry

1 cup grated Cheddar cheese

¼ cup finely-chopped olives

1 finely-chopped spring onion stem

½ tsp dried oregano

1 clove garlic, chopped fine

¼ cup melted butter

Method

In a small bowl, combine cheese, olives, spring onion, oregano and garlic; set aside.

Lightly grease a baking tray and preheat the oven to 375°F/190°C/Gas Mark 5. Place one sheet of phyllo pastry on a flat surface. Cover remaining sheets with a damp cloth to prevent them from drying out. Brush the pastry with melted butter. Top with 2 more phyllo sheets, brushing each one with butter. Spoon half the cheese mixture in the centre and carefully roll up into a tight roll.

Place seam side down on the prepared baking tray. Brush the top with butter. Repeat with remaining phyllo sheets and filling. Bake for 10-15 minutes until golden brown. Cut each roll into 1-1½-inch lengths and serve warm.

Makes 16-20 servings

Mediterranean Pizza

Ingredients

4 (6-inch) pita breads

Garlic-flavoured olive oil to brush the bread

1 cup Hummus (Page 101)

1 tbsp freshly-chopped basil

½ cup (each) sliced red or yellow capsicums and olives

¼ cup slivered sun-dried tomatoes

100 gm (each) feta cheese and mozzarella cheese

To serve

Chilli flakes, dried oregano and thyme

Method

Brush pita loaves with olive oil and toast them in the oven until crisp. Remove and spread ¼ cup hummus evenly on each. Sprinkle basil, capsicums, olives and sun-dried tomatoes all over on each pita bread. Mix both kinds of cheese and spread evenly on each loaf.

Bake in an oven at 400°F/200°C/Gas Mark 6 for 4–5 minutes.

Place on cutting board, cut into wedges and serve with chilli flakes and herbs.

Serves } 4–6

Smoked Cottage Cheese and Red Pepper Shots

Ingredients

400 gm cottage cheese, cut into ½ inch cubes

2 tbsp olive oil

1 tbsp dried mixed herbs

Salt and pepper to taste

½ cup cream cheese spread

2 medium red capsicums halved and grilled

1 tbsp toasted and chopped walnuts or pine nuts

Salt and chilli flakes to taste

A piece of charcoal and a teaspoon oil to smoke the cheese

To garnish

Freshly-chopped herbs

To serve

Thin breadsticks, crackers or Melba Toast (Page 217)

Method

Place cottage cheese pieces in a bowl with 1 tbsp olive oil, herbs, salt and pepper. Toss gently to coat. Set aside for 20 minutes.

Heat remaining 1 tbsp of olive oil in a heavy frying pan. Add prepared cottage cheese and cook for 3-4 minutes. Push the cheese towards the rim of the pan and make place for a small bowl in the centre. Place burning charcoal in the bowl; gently pour 1 tsp oil over it. As soon as it starts to smoke, cover the pan with a lid to arrest the smoke. Keep it covered for 1-2 minutes or until the smoke dies down. Open the lid and allow cheese to cool. Transfer cottage cheese to a liquidizer jar and blend along with cream cheese spread until smooth.

Peel the skin from the grilled capsicums and coarsely chop them. Add walnuts or pine nuts, salt and chilli flakes to taste. Set aside.

Take a shot glass, fill ¾ with cheese mixture and top it with capsicum mixture. Garnish with herbs and serve with breadsticks, crackers or Melba toast.

Serves } 12

Middle-eastern Wrap with Tahina Dressing

Ingredients

4 loaves wholewheat pita bread

½ cup Hummus (Page 101)

For the filling

1 cup cooked rice

¼ cup feta cheese cubes

¼ cup toasted pine nuts

¼ cup thinly-sliced sun-dried tomatoes

½ cup broccoli, chopped

½ medium red or yellow capsicum, diced

1 spring onion stem, sliced

1 tbsp olive oil

1 tbsp freshly-chopped basil

Salt and pepper to taste

For the tahina dressing

¼ cup tahina paste

¼ cup thick yogurt

4 cloves garlic, crushed

2 small green chillies, finely chopped

Juice of 1 lemon

Salt to taste

Method

Mix together rice, pine nuts, feta cheese, sun-dried tomatoes, broccoli, capsicum, spring onion, olive oil, basil, salt and pepper. Toss gently to mix and place in a refrigerator to chill.

In a separate bowl, combine all the ingredients for the dressing. Just before serving, add the dressing to the rice mixture and toss gently to mix.

Warm the pita breads and spread hummus evenly on each one. Spoon the rice mixture over and roll up. Serve immediately.

Serves } 4

Note: You can use lettuce leaves or tortillas instead of pita bread.

Gyros

Greek-style Sandwich

Ingredients

6 loaves thin pita bread, slit

2-3 cups shredded iceberg lettuce

1 medium onion, thinly sliced

2 medium tomatoes, roughly chopped

1 medium cucumber, thinly sliced

¼ cup sliced black olives (optional)

1½ cups Tzatziki (Page 98)

1 cup cottage cheese, crumbled or cubed

1 tbsp seasoning (recipe follows)

1 tsp crushed garlic

1 tsp vinegar

2 tbsp olive oil

Salt, pepper and paprika to taste

For the seasoning

1½ tbsp paprika

½ tbsp salt

½ tbsp pepper

½ tbsp oregano

½ tbsp basil

½ tsp nutmeg

½ tsp cumin powder

Note: Traditionally 3-4 French fries are placed on top of the sandwich.

Method

Mix all the seasoning ingredients in a small bowl and fill in an airtight jar.

Place cottage cheese in a bowl and sprinkle 1 tbsp seasoning mix, crushed garlic, vinegar and olive oil. Mix well and set aside for 5-10 minutes. Cook the mixture over medium heat till a little dry. Remove from heat and set aside.

To assemble gyros

Heat pita bread slightly on a hot griddle. Place it on a work surface. Arrange lettuce, onion, tomatoes, cucumber and olives if using. (Approx. ½ cup salad for each gyros). Season with salt and pepper. Spoon the cottage cheese mixture over the salad. Top with tzatziki and fold into a cone-shaped sandwich. Sprinkle additional paprika if required. Serve immediately.

Serves } 6

Tzatziki

Greek-style Cucumber Dip

Ingredients

2 cups thick yogurt

1 medium cucumber, grated and drained

3-4 cloves garlic, crushed

1 tbsp chopped dill

4 tbsp olive oil

2 tbsp vinegar

Salt and pepper to taste

To garnish
Sprigs of parsley

To serve
Crisp pita bread

Method

Mix yogurt, cucumber, garlic and dill in a bowl. Pour in olive oil and vinegar alternately, mixing continuously. Season to taste. Garnish with the parsley and chill. Serve tzatziki as an appetiser with crisp pita bread or use it as a filling in sandwiches.

Makes 2½ cups

Hummus Croustades

Ingredients

24-26 croustades cases (readymade)

1 cup smooth Hummus (Page 101)

½ cup prepared couscous

1 tbsp (each) olive oil and freshly-chopped parsley

1 tsp chilli flakes

Salt to taste

To garnish

Sliced black olives and paprika

Method

Heat croustades cases in the oven till slightly crisp and store in airtight container.

Prepare hummus, chill for 30 minutes and fill in piping bag.

Toss couscous with olive oil, parsley, chilli flakes and salt. Line the croustades cases with 1 tsp of prepared couscous. Pipe the hummus in a swirl over the couscous. Garnish with paprika and sliced olives. Serve immediately.

Makes 24-26 croustades

Layered Hummus Dip

Ingredients

1 recipe Hummus (Page 101)

White layer

200 gm feta cheese

1 tbsp parsley

1 tbsp basil

1 tbsp crushed garlic

Red layer

2 tbsp red chilli paste

1 tbsp olive oil

Salt to taste

Green layer

1 cup fresh basil leaves, plucked and washed

1 tbsp pine nuts, toasted

2-3 cloves garlic

1 tsp pepper

¼ cup olive oil

1 tsp salt

To serve

Crisp pita bread triangles

Method

For the white layer, crumble the cheese in a small bowl and add the herbs and garlic.

For the red layer, in a separate bowl, mix together the chilli paste, oil and salt.

In a small blender jar, place all the ingredients for the green layer and blend until smooth. Transfer to a small bowl.

To assemble the dip

Take a 3-cup capacity transparent, glass serving bowl. Divide hummus into 3 equal portions. Spread one portion evenly at the bottom of the bowl. Spread the green layer evenly over it. Top with a layer of hummus, followed by the white layer. Spread a layer of hummus again and over it the red layer. Chill for half an hour and serve with crisp pita bread triangles.

Serves } 6

Hummus

Ingredients

250 gm chickpeas

A pinch of soda

3-4 tbsp tahina paste

Salt to taste

3-4 tbsp lemon juice

6-8 cloves garlic

1 tbsp finely-chopped parsley

1 tbsp finely-chopped basil (optional)

To garnish

Olive oil and paprika

Method

Soak the chickpeas in water for 6 hours with a pinch of soda. Cook in a pressure cooker until very soft. Drain and set aside to cool. Reserve the water from the cooker. Place the chickpeas in a food processor with tahina paste, salt, lemon juice, garlic, parsley and basil. Process till you get a thick paste. Add about 3-4 tbsp of reserved water from the cooker if the mixture is too dry. Transfer the ground paste to a serving bowl and adjust the salt and lemon juice. This will give you basic hummus.

Use this for layered hummus or serve it separately as a dip. Ladle the hummus into a bowl and make a design on top with a fork. Pour olive oil over and sprinkle with paprika. Serve at room temperature with pita bread.

Spiced Sweet Roasted Red Pepper and Feta Hummus

Ingredients

200 gm chickpeas, soaked overnight and boiled

200 gm red capsicum, roasted and peeled

½ cup crumbled feta cheese

3 tbsp lemon juice

1½ tbsp tahina paste

1 large clove garlic, crushed

½ tsp (each) cumin powder, chilli powder and salt

To garnish

A few whole chickpeas, olive oil and freshly chopped parsley

To serve

Crisp pita bread

Method

In an electric blender or food processor, purée the chickpeas, red capsicum, feta, lemon juice, tahina, garlic, cumin, chilli powder and salt. Process until the mixture is smooth and slightly fluffy. Transfer to a bowl and refrigerate for at least 1 hour.

Remove from fridge and make a dent in the centre, pour olive oil and sprinkle whole chickpeas and parsley over. Serve with pita bread.

Makes 2 cups

Red Pepper Hummus

Ingredients

200 gm chickpeas, soaked overnight and boiled

4-5 tbsp tahina

4-5 tbsp lemon juice

2 cloves garlic

2 medium red capsicums, roasted and peeled

½ tsp dried basil

Salt and pepper to taste

To garnish

Olive oil, chilli flakes and fresh basil leaves

To serve

Crisp pita triangles

Method

Process all the ingredients together in a blender until smooth. Pour out into a serving bowl and make a design with a fork and drizzle olive oil. Sprinkle chilli flakes and decorate with basil leaves. Serve at room temperature with crisp pita bread.

Serves } 6

Muttabal

Greek Eggplant Dip

Ingredients

2 medium eggplants, roasted

3 medium tomatoes, coarsely chopped

2 cloves garlic, finely chopped

1 tbsp finely-chopped parsley

1 medium onion, finely chopped

1 tsp salt

1 tsp sugar

¼ tsp pepper

Juice of 1 lemon

To garnish
Olive oil and chilli flakes

To serve
Crisp pita triangles

Method

Hold the roasted eggplant under running cold water and then remove the skin. Place the eggplant on a board and chop coarsely. Add the rest of the ingredients and transfer to a serving bowl. Make designs on the surface with a fork, drizzle olive oil and sprinkle chilli flakes. Serve cold or at room temperature with crisp pita triangles.

Serves } 4–6

Mediterranean Dip Platter

Ingredients

For jalapeño hummus

100 gm chickpeas, soaked and boiled

2 tbsp tahina paste

2 tbsp olive oil

2 tbsp lemon juice

2-3 cloves garlic

1 tbsp finely-chopped jalapeño chillies

Salt to taste

For pickled eggplant relish

200 gm large or small eggplants, diced

2 tbsp olive oil

2 cloves garlic, crushed with little salt

2 tbsp vinegar

2 tbsp chopped parsley

1 tsp chilli flakes

1 tsp salt

1 tsp sugar

For creamy pesto dip

¾ cup cream cheese, softened

¼ cup whipped cream

Green pesto sauce

1-2 tbsp Parmesan cheese

To garnish

Olive oil, sliced olives and pine nuts

For muhammara

2 medium red capsicums, roasted and skin removed

2 tbsp pine nuts

2 tbsp pomegranate juice

1 tbsp lemon juice

1 tbsp sugar

2-3 cloves garlic, crushed with 1 tsp salt

3 tbsp fresh breadcrumbs

3 tbsp olive oil

1 tsp salt

1 tsp chilli flakes

1 tsp cumin powder

To garnish

Olive oil and chilli flakes

To serve

Crisp pita bread triangles

Method

Jalapeño Hummus

Place all the ingredients in a blender and blend until smooth. If the mixture feels dry, add a little water. Pour into a serving bowl and garnish with olive oil and chopped jalapeño chillies.

Pickled Eggplant Relish

Sprinkle a little salt over chopped eggplant and set aside for 30 minutes. Heat 1 tbsp oil in a frying pan and sauté the eggplant until soft. Transfer to a bowl. Add the remaining ingredients, mix well and set aside for 2-3 hours. Garnish with remaining oil and chilli flakes.

Creamy Pesto Dip

Process all the ingredients in a blender and turn out into a serving bowl. Garnish with olive oil, olives and pine nuts.

Muhammara

Mix all the ingredients in a blender and blend until smooth. Turn out into a bowl, garnish with olive oil and chilli flakes.

To serve

Arrange all the bowls on a platter or large tray and serve with a basket of crisp pita bread or lavash.

Rice with Chickpeas

Ingredients

1 cup raw rice

½ cup chickpeas, soaked and boiled

1½ tsp salt

1 tbsp olive oil

2 tbsp butter

1 medium onion, finely sliced

1 large tomato, blanched and chopped

3-4 tbsp pine nuts, toasted

2 tbsp mixed fresh herbs (tarragon, chives, parsley, thyme, dill)

½ tsp cumin powder or cinnamon powder

1 tsp pepper

To serve

Middle-eastern Delight (recipe follows)

Note: This mixture is also used to stuff vegetables like large eggplants, capsicums, courgettes or tomatoes. The quantity is sufficient to stuff 1 kg of vegetables.

Method

Cook the rice in two cups of boiling water to which ½ tsp of salt has been added till just done. Remove from heat, add the olive oil and toss gently with a fork.

In a wide pan, melt butter and sauté onion until soft. Add the tomato, pine nuts, herbs, cumin or cinnamon, 1 tsp salt and pepper. Cook till tomatoes are slightly soft, but not too mushy. Add boiled chickpeas and the rice and stir gently to mix. Adjust seasonings and serve hot with Middle-eastern Delight.

Serves } 4-6

Middle-eastern Delight

Combine ½ cup salad oil, ¼ cup soy sauce, 3 tbsp wine vinegar, 1½ tbsp Worcestershire sauce, 2 tsp dry mustard powder, ¾ tsp salt, 1 crushed clove garlic, ½ tsp dried parsley, 1 tsp black pepper and 5 tbsp lemon juice in a blender and process till smooth. Pour into a jar and store in the refrigerator until ready to use.

Makes 1 cup

Curried Cheese Mousse

Ingredients

200 gm feta cheese

2 tsp unflavoured gelatine

¼ cup vegetable stock made with ¼ cup water and ¼ stock cube

1 tbsp olive oil

½ cup finely-chopped onions

1-2 cloves garlic, chopped

1 tbsp wine vinegar

½ tsp curry powder

½ tsp salt

½ tsp pepper

½ tsp mustard

½ cup beaten fresh cream (measured after beating)

To garnish

Cherry tomatoes, iceberg lettuce leaves and freshly-chopped herbs

To serve

Salted crackers

Method

Dissolve the gelatine in the vegetable stock.

Heat the oil in a small pan and cook onion and garlic until transparent. Pour the gelatine mixture onto the onions and bring to a boil. Lower the heat and simmer for 2 minutes. Pour into a chilled bowl and leave the mixture to set.

Place the chilled mixture in a blender with feta cheese, vinegar, curry powder, salt, pepper, mustard and ¼ cup boiling water and process until smooth.

Transfer the mixture to a bowl and fold in the cream. Pour into 2 ramekins (small dishes) and chill well.

Garnish with tomatoes, lettuce and herbs. Serve with crackers.

Serves } 4–6

Vegetable Tajine with Couscous

Ingredients

250 gm mixed vegetables (such as zucchini, babycorn, eggplant, onion etc), cut into cubes

1 cup packaged couscous or any thick variety of rice

½ cup olive oil

¼ cup freshly-chopped parsley

3 tbsp chopped coriander leaves

5-6 large cloves garlic, chopped

1 tbsp mild paprika powder

2 tsp cumin powder

¼ cup white or fava beans, soaked overnight and boiled

1 medium onion, thinly sliced

500 gm tomatoes, blanched and chopped

1 medium red capsicum, thinly sliced

1 lemon, thinly sliced

1 tsp salt

1 tsp pepper

½ cup sliced black or green olives

To garnish

Freshly-chopped herbs, such as parsley, basil etc

A few saffron threads, soaked in a little hot water

Method

Mix olive oil, parsley, coriander leaves, garlic, paprika and cumin powder in a bowl. Toss chopped vegetables and fava beans into this mixture and marinate for 2 hours, turning occasionally.

Preheat the oven to 350°F/180°C/Gas Mark 4.

In a tajine or a baking dish arrange half the onions, tomatoes, capsicum and lemon. Drain the vegetables from the marinade and arrange them over onion and tomatoes. Reserve the marinade liquid. Season with half the salt and pepper. Top with remaining onion, tomatoes, lemon and capsicum. Season with the remaining salt and pepper. Arrange sliced olives on top and pour the reserved marinade all over. Cover the dish with a lid or foil paper.

Bake for 30-35 minutes. Garnish with fresh herbs and saffron.

Cook the couscous according to the instructions on the packet or cook the rice and serve with the hot tajine.

Serves } 6

Penne and Asparagus with Muhammara Sauce

Ingredients

250 gm penne, boiled and drained*

200 gm fresh asparagus cut into 2-inch lengths and blanched

1 tbsp olive oil

2 cloves garlic, crushed

1 tbsp chopped basil

1 tsp chilli flakes

Salt to taste

For muhammara sauce

1 medium red capsicum, cut into quarters and roasted

3 tbsp toasted pine nuts or walnuts

⅓ cup (each) olive oil and bread crumbs

1 tsp sumac

2 cloves garlic, crushed with little salt

½ tsp salt

½ tsp pepper

½ tsp cumin powder

1 tsp chilli flakes

*reserve a little of the liquid to thin the sauce

To serve

Grated Parmesan cheese

Method

For the pasta

Heat oil in a wide pan; add garlic, basil and chilli flakes. Add the pasta, asparagus and salt. Set aside.

For muhammara sauce

Blend all the ingredients in a blender to a smooth purée.

Just before serving, gently toss the pasta in the muhammara sauce. Add a little pasta water if the sauce is too thick. Garnish with Parmesan cheese and serve hot.

Serves } 6-8

Spinach and Cream Pie

Spankópita me Kréma

Ingredients

For the pastry

250 gm plain flour

¼ tsp salt

¼ tsp baking powder

100 gm butter

2-3 tbsp cream

For the filling

500 gm spinach leaves, cleaned, washed and chopped

2-3 spring onions stems, finely chopped

2-3 tbsp chopped dill

2-3 tbsp olive oil

2-3 tbsp plain flour

Salt, pepper and nutmeg to taste

½ cup milk

½ cup cream

½ cup feta cheese, crumbled

Method

For the pastry

Sift the flour, salt and baking powder together. Rub butter into the flour so that it resembles breadcrumbs. Add the cream and enough water to make soft dough. Cover and chill for 10 minutes.

Roll out half the dough and line an 8-inch pie dish with the pastry. Bake it at 350°F/180°C/Gas Mark 4 for 20 minutes. Remove from the oven and set aside to cool. Roll out the remaining dough for the top covering and set aside.

For the filling

Heat olive oil and sauté spinach leaves and onions for 5 minutes, or until slightly wilted. Add flour, salt, pepper and nutmeg.

In a small bowl, mix together milk, cream, dill and crumbled feta cheese and beat until smooth. Fold into the spinach mixture and pour into the pie shell. Cover the top with the rolled-out pastry and prick it with a knife.

Bake it in an oven at 350°F/180°C/Gas Mark 4 for 20-25 minutes or until the top is golden. Remove from the oven and cool for 5-7 minutes before serving.

Serves } 6-8

Vegetable Kibbeh Pie

Ingredients

1 cup bulgar wheat, washed and soaked in water

2 cups mashed potatoes

1 tsp dried parsley

Salt and pepper to taste

1 tbsp olive oil

For the filling

2 tbsp olive oil

½ cup (each) chopped and cooked spinach & boiled brown lentils

1 tsp (each) cumin and chilli powder

¼ cup (each) fried onions and chopped walnuts

2 tbsp (each) finely-chopped coriander and mint

Salt to taste

To garnish

Sprig of parsley and halved walnuts

To serve

Green salad and Ayran (recipe follows)

Method

For the filling

Heat olive oil in a frying pan; add spinach, lentils, cumin, chilli powder and salt. Cook for 2 minutes. Remove from stove and add onions, walnuts, coriander and mint. Mix well.

Mix together mashed potatoes, drained bulgar wheat, parsley, salt and pepper. Heat 1 tbsp olive oil in a skillet; spread half the mixture pressing evenly. Top it evenly with spinach-lentil mixture.

Take remaining potato mixture; flatten it to fit over the spinach mixture, pressing gently to cover the top. Brush it lightly with oil. Place it on a medium heat and cook until both sides are golden brown. Remove from pan and cut into wedges, garnish with sprig of parsley and walnuts. Serve with green salad and ayran.

Serves } 6–8

Ayran

Mix together 1 cup yogurt, 1 cup chilled water, ½ tsp each of cumin powder and salt, 1 tbsp chopped mint and ice. Serve in a small glass.

Greek Country Salad (recipe on page 85)

Mediterranean Pizza (recipe on page 94)

Moussaka with Aubergines

Moussakás me Melitzánes

Ingredients

2 large aubergines

2-3 tomatoes, chopped

2-3 tbsp olive oil

1 medium onion, finely chopped

1 tsp finely-chopped garlic

1 bay leaf

1 tsp Spice Mixture (recipe follows)

250 gm crumbled cottage cheese or feta cheese

Salt and pepper to taste

Refined flour

1½ cups Béchamel Sauce (recipe follows)

¼ cup grated Parmesan cheese

Oil for deep-frying

Method

Wash and trim the stem of the aubergines. Cut into thick slices and soak in salted water for 1 hour. Drain the aubergine slices and discard excess water. Roll the slices in the flour and deep-fry them in hot oil. Drain on kitchen paper.

Heat oil in a saucepan and sauté onion, garlic and bay leaf for 2-3 minutes. Add ½ tsp of spice mix and cook for another 1 minute. Remove from heat and stir in the tomatoes, cottage cheese, salt and pepper. Set aside.

Grease a baking dish with a little oil and arrange half of the aubergine slices at the bottom. Top with half the cottage cheese mixture and repeat the layers once more. Finally pour béchamel sauce over the last layer. Sprinkle with grated Parmesan cheese and bake at 400°F/200°C/Gas Mark 6 for 20-25 minutes. Cut into squares and serve hot.

Spice Mixture

Mix together 2 tbsp oregano with 1 tbsp each of cinnamon powder, clove powder and nutmeg powder. Store in an airtight jar.

Béchamel Sauce (Sáltsa Kréma Bessamél)
Heat ¼ cup oil in a pan, stir in ¼ cup plain flour and cook over medium heat for 5 minutes. Add ¾ cup milk and ¼ cup cream, whisking continuously. Add ¼ tsp each of salt, pepper and nutmeg. Cook for 5 minutes stirring all the time. Finally add ¼ cup grated Parmesan cheese. If the sauce is too thick add a little more milk.

Makes 1½ cups

Spanish Tapas
(recipe on page 115)

Stuffed Peppers and Tomatoes

Domátes ke Piperiés Yemistés

Ingredients

6 medium tomatoes

3 medium yellow, red or green capsicums

2 medium potatoes

Salt and pepper to taste

1 tbsp sugar

Juice of 2 tomatoes

3 tbsp olive oil

For the filling

¼ cup olive oil

2 medium onions, finely chopped

250 gm raw rice, washed and soaked

3 tbsp finely-chopped parsley

1 tsp chopped mint

Salt and pepper to taste

1 tsp paprika

Method

Peel and slice the potatoes and sauté in 3 tbsp olive oil. Wash the tomatoes and capsicums. Using a sharp knife, cut a thin, round slice off the stem end of each one and set aside to use later as a lid. Remove seeds from capsicums and discard them. Remove pulp from tomatoes and chop the pulp finely (you should have around 3 tbsp). Arrange the hollowed out tomatoes and capsicums in a baking dish, season with salt and pepper and sprinkle a little sugar in each tomato. Arrange potato slices around the capsicums and tomatoes.

For the filling

In a wide pan, heat oil and sauté onions till pale gold. Add washed rice, parsley, mint, salt, pepper and 2-2½ cups water. Cook until rice is tender. Add the chopped tomato pulp and paprika. Fill the tomatoes and capsicums with this filling till three-fourth full. Cover them with reserved tops. Place in a baking dish. Mix together the tomato juice and olive oil and pour all around the vegetables. Bake at 350°F/180°C/Gas Mark 4 for 30-35 minutes.

Serves } 6-8

Escalibada

Red Pepper and Aubergine Salad

Ingredients

4 medium red capsicums

3 thin long aubergines (eggplants/ brinjals)

1 large onion and tomato each

4 medium potatoes

½ cup olive oil

6 tsp vinegar

2 cloves garlic, chopped

Salt and pepper to taste

Method

Preheat the oven to 350°F/180°C/Gas Mark 4.

Wash and wipe all the vegetables dry and place them on a baking tray in the oven. Wrap the potatoes in foil and place them in the oven as well. Bake for 30 minutes, turning the vegetables and potatoes over once in-between.

Remove from the oven and peel all the vegetables while still hot. Remove the stems of capsicums and aubergines and cut them into long strips. Slice the onion and tomato. Cut the potatoes in half and scoop out a little pulp keeping the skin intact. Arrange all the vegetables on a serving platter.

In a small bowl, mix together the garlic, olive oil, vinegar, salt and pepper. Dribble over the salad. Serve cold.

Serves | 4

Patatas Bravas

Ingredients

3 medium potatoes

Oil for deep frying

3 medium tomatoes, peeled and deseeded

A few drops of vinegar

1 tsp plain flour

Salt to taste

1 tsp Spanish paprika

Method

Peel the potatoes, cut them into small pieces and deep-fry them over a low heat until golden.

Heat 1 tsp oil in a saucepan and add tomatoes. Cook, stirring and crushing with a spoon continuously, till soft and pulpy. Add the vinegar, flour, salt and paprika and mix well.

Place hot potatoes on a serving dish and pour the sauce over and serve warm or cold.

Serves } 4

Marinated Olives

Ingredients

1 cup olives, deseeded or ready sliced

2 dried red chillies, finely-chopped

or

1 tsp crushed fresh red chillies

12 cloves garlic, finely chopped

1 tbsp olive oil

½ tsp dried oregano

1 tsp chopped basil

Red vinegar and a dash of lemon juice

Method

Crush the olives lightly and toss them with the rest of the ingredients in a bowl. Set aside for 3-4 hours before using.

Serves } 4

Chickpea and Spinach Tapas

Ingredients

2 cups chickpeas

2-3 bunches (350 gm) fresh spinach

1 medium red capsicum, finely chopped

2 medium tomatoes, blanched and chopped

4 cloves garlic, crushed

2 tbsp finely-chopped coriander leaves

1 tbsp finely-chopped chives

Juice of 2 lemons

¼ cup virgin olive oil

Salt and pepper to taste

Method

Soak the chickpeas overnight and cook till tender and set aside to cool.

Wash and cook the spinach with a little oil in a frying pan till slightly wilted. Finely chop the spinach.

Mix all the ingredients in a bowl and toss together with the spinach. Chill in the refrigerator for 2 hours.

Serve cold with toasted bread or as a salad.

Serves } 4

Aioli Sauce

Ingredients

6 large cloves garlic

½ cup Mayonnaise (Page 244)

1½ tbsp lemon juice

¼ cup olive oil

Salt to taste

Method

Process all the ingredients in a blender. Store in an airtight jar in a refrigerator.

Makes 1 cup

Pita Bread

Ingredients

225 gm wholewheat flour

½ tsp (each) salt and brown sugar

1 tbsp dry yeast

½ cup warm water

1 tbsp olive oil

Method

Sift the flour and salt together in a bowl. Sprinkle yeast and sugar over warm water. Cover and set aside in a warm place for 20 minutes or until frothy. Add this to the flour mixture. Make soft dough. Turn it out on a floured board and knead until the dough is elastic and smooth. Pour olive oil in a bowl and place the dough over it, cover and set aside in a warm place for 40 minutes or until double in size. Punch down the dough on a lightly floured surface and knead until oil is absorbed.

Preheat the oven to 400°F/200°C/Gas Mark 6. Divide the dough into 8 equal portions for small pita and 4 portions for large ones. Roll each portion into oval shape about ¼" thick. Place it on greased baking sheet and bake in the pre-heated oven for 7-10 minutes until well risen. Remove from the baking sheet and cool on a wire rack. Use as required.

Makes 4 large or 8 small loaves

Khobz

Moroccan Pita Bread

Ingredients

200 gm wholewheat flour

3 tbsp maize flour

½ tsp (each) salt, paprika and brown sugar

1 tbsp dry yeast

½ cup warm water

1 tbsp olive oil

2 tbsp toasted sesame seeds

Method

Sift the two kinds of flour, paprika and salt together in a bowl. Sprinkle yeast and sugar over warm water. Cover and set aside in a warm place for 20 minutes or until frothy. Add this to the flour mixture. Make soft dough. Turn it out on a floured board and knead until the dough is elastic and smooth. Pour olive oil in a bowl and place the dough over it, cover and set aside in a warm place for 40 minutes or until double in size. Punch down the dough on a lightly floured surface and knead until oil is absorbed.

Preheat the oven to 400°F/200°C/Gas Mark 6. Divide the dough into 8 equal portions for small pita and 4 portions for large ones. Roll each portion into oval shape about ¼" thick. Place it on greased baking sheet. Press sesame seeds on each portion and bake in the preheated oven for 7-10 minutes until well risen. Remove from the baking sheet and cool on a wire rack. Use as required.

Makes 4 large or 8 small loaves.

Dukkah

Egyptian Spice Blend

Ingredients

$^{2}/_{3}$ cup hazelnuts

½ cup sesame seeds

2 tbsp (each) coriander seeds, cumin seeds and black pepper

1 tsp sea salt or rock salt

Method

Place hazelnuts on a baking sheet in the oven and bake at 350°F/180°C/Gas Mark 4 for about 5 minutes. Remove and set aside to cool.

In a dry skillet, roast sesame seeds over medium heat until light golden brown. Remove and set aside in a bowl.

In the same skillet, toast coriander and cumin seeds till they begin to pop. Transfer to a grinder and powder them. Pour this into the bowl with sesame seeds.

Place the cooled hazelnuts in a food processor or grinder and process until finely ground. Stir into the bowl with spices. Add salt and pepper and mix well.

Serve it with toasted crusty bread, and olive oil. Dip bread into olive oil, then into dukkah and enjoy this unique mix.

Makes 1½ cups

Mexican

Hola! Welcome to a land of marvellous flavours, appetising colours and unmatched tastes. Though corn and beans are staple ingredients in their food, Mexicans love bell peppers, squash, potatoes, avocados and tomatoes. Tuck into spicy salsas like the Habanero and Red Salsa, delicious dips such as Asparagus Guacamole and Jalapeño Chilli Jam and favourites such as Nachos, Tacos, Quesadillas and Enchiladas...

Mexican Corn Soup

Ingredients

2 cups corn kernels

1 cup Vegetable Stock (Page 245)

3 tbsp butter

½ cup finely-chopped spring onion

½ cup finely-chopped red capsicum

2 cloves garlic crushed with ½ tsp salt

3 cups milk

Salt and pepper to taste

To garnish

2 tbsp finely-chopped parsley

6 tbsp Sour Cream (Page 245)

3 tbsp finely-chopped jalapeño chillies.

Method

Combine corn kernels and stock and process in a blender to a smooth purée.

Melt the butter in a saucepan; wilt the spring onion, capsicum and garlic. Add milk, salt and pepper. Cook for fifteen minutes over low heat.

Divide the hot soup among six bowls and garnish individually with parsley, sour cream and jalapeño chillies.

Serves 6

Cream of Chilli Soup

Ingredients

3-4 jalapeño chillies, chopped

¼ cup fresh cream

2 large corn tortillas cut into ¼ inch-wide strips

3 tbsp butter

1 cup chopped onion

1 clove garlic

½ tsp oregano

1 bay leaf

2 cups Vegetable Stock (Page 245)

1 medium potato, peeled and cubed

Salt and pepper to taste

1 cup Monterey Jack or mozzarella cheese, grated

Method

Cook the tortillas in a hot oven till crisp.

In a saucepan, melt butter. Add onion, garlic, oregano and bay leaf. Cook until onions are soft. Stir in the stock, potato, salt and pepper. Bring to a boil and simmer till potato is tender. Remove from heat and set aside to cool.

Discard the bay leaf and purée the soup in a blender. Put through a sieve and return to heat. Add the chillies and simmer for ten minutes. Adjust the seasoning and add the cream. Set aside until ready to serve.

Reheat gently just before serving. Add the cheese and ladle the soup into individual bowls. Sprinkle tortilla chips and serve immediately.

Serves } 4

Chilled Avocado and Mint Soup

Ingredients

4 cups diced ripe avocado

5 tbsp lemon juice

¼ cup finely-chopped spring onions

¼ cup coriander leaves

1 tsp chopped jalapeño chilli

3 cups thin Vegetable Stock (Page 245)

3 cups chilled buttermilk

Salt and pepper to taste

¼ cup thick cream

To garnish

Chopped tomato and mint leaves

Method

Peel and chop the avocado only when you are ready to make it. Drizzle lemon juice over the avocado while cutting.

Place all the ingredients except the cream, in a blender jar and process till mixed. Pour into a stainless steel bowl, add the cream and chill in the freezer till ready to serve.

Garnish with tomatoes and mint. Serve over a bowl of ice.

Serves } 4–6

Tomatillo and Pepita Soup

Ingredients

¼ cup unsalted shelled pepitas (pumpkin seeds)

1 kg tomatillos (green tomatoes)

1-2 jalapeño chilies

1 head garlic

2 tbsp olive oil

2 cups Vegetable Stock (Page 245)

1 medium avocado, peeled and diced (optional)

⅓ cup finely-chopped spring onion

¼ cup finely-chopped cilantro

½ cup halved cherry tomatoes

Salt and pepper to taste

To garnish

Coarsely-grated cheese and sprigs of cilantro

Method

Finely grind the pepitas in the grinder. Brush the tomatillos and jalapeños with oil and place them under the grill until slightly charred. Peel them and add half the tomatillos, jalapeños and 1 cup stock to the grinder jar with pumpkin seeds. Roast whole head of garlic and press the shell to squeeze out the pulp. Add this to blender with tomatillos and process to make a coarse purée.

Transfer to a pan and add vegetable stock, salt and pepper. If you feel the soup is too thick, simply add a little water to obtain the right consistency. Chop the remaining tomatoes and add to the purée. Add remaining ingredients and heat it through.

If you wish to serve this cold, transfer the soup to a bowl after the first boil and chill for 2-3 hours. For hot soup, ladle soup in individual bowls, garnish with cheese and cilantro and serve with warm corn bread.

Serves } 6-8

Mexican Potato Salad

Ingredients

1 kg potatoes, boiled, peeled and cut into cubes

1 cup yellow corn kernels, boiled

2 tomatoes, blanched and chopped

1 bunch spring onions, finely chopped

½ cup Red Salsa (Page 135)

2 tbsp finely-chopped coriander leaves

2 tbsp lemon juice

2 tbsp finely-chopped jalapeño peppers

Salt and pepper to taste

1 tsp taco seasoning

To garnish

2 tbsp finely-grated cheese, ¼ cup Sour Cream (Page 245)

Method

Mix together potatoes, corn, tomatoes and spring onions in a bowl.

In a separate small bowl, mix salsa, coriander, lemon juice, jalapeños, salt, pepper and taco seasoning. Add to the vegetables and toss gently.

Garnish and serve at once or chill overnight.

Serves } 6

Fiesta Corn Salad

Ingredients

400 gm yellow corn kernels, boiled

2 tbsp olive oil

Salt and pepper to taste

2 tbsp vinegar

2 tbsp taco seasoning

1½ cups blanched and diced tomatoes

½ cup sliced olives

½ cup diced red or green capsicum

½ cup spring onions

¼ cup finely-chopped jalapeño chillies

To garnish
Finely-chopped coriander leaves

To serve
Sour Cream (Page 245) and crushed taco chips

Method

In a bowl, mix together olive oil, salt, pepper, vinegar and taco seasoning. Add the rest of the ingredients and toss gently to mix. Cover with cling film and chill for several hours.

Garnish with coriander and serve with sour cream and crushed chips.

Serves } 6

Black Bean, Corn, Potato and Pepper Salad

Ingredients

For the salad

½ cup black beans, soaked overnight and boiled

½ cup boiled yellow corn

100 gm baby potatoes boiled and peeled

100 gm baby onions, boiled and peeled

½ tsp dried thyme

½ tsp oregano

Salt to taste

1 medium onion finely chopped

1 medium tomato finely chopped

½ cup cubed red capsicum

½ cup cubed green capsicum

For the dressing

1 tsp crushed garlic

½ tsp pepper

1 tbsp lemon juice

1 tbsp cider vinegar

1 tbsp finely-chopped jalapeño chilli

½ tsp cumin powder

½ tsp paprika

1 tsp grated lemon rind

5-6 tbsp olive oil

1 tsp salt

1 tbsp finely-chopped mint

1 tbsp finely-chopped coriander

To garnish

Sprigs of mint and coriander leaves

Method

Boil the beans with thyme, oregano and salt until soft, but firm. Drain and set aside.

Mix the remaining ingredients in a bowl and set aside.

Prepare the dressing by blending all the ingredients together in a blender. Toss the prepared vegetables with the dressing and add the beans. Adjust salt.

Garnish with coriander and mint sprigs. Serve chilled or at room temperature.

Serves } 4-6

Sizzling Vegetable Fajitas
(recipe on page 157)

A ROSA #42

Southwestern Salad with Avocado Dressing

Ingredients

For the salad

1 cup chopped tomatoes

½ cup chopped white onion

¼ cup sliced jalapeño chillies

½ cup chopped capsicum (red, yellow or green)

2 cups shredded lettuce or salad greens

¼ cup grated cheese

For the dressing

1 medium ripe avocado

3-4 tbsp lemon juice

2 cloves garlic, crushed

1 tbsp mustard paste

2 tbsp finely-chopped coriander

2 tbsp balsamic vinegar

2 tbsp finely-chopped jalapeño chillies

⅓ cup olive oil

½-¾ cup ice water

Salt, pepper and cumin powder to taste

To garnish

2-3 slices of avocado and a sprig of coriander.

Method

For the salad
Place the vegetables in a large bowl, cover with cling film and chill thoroughly.

For the dressing
Mash the avocado and drizzle lemon juice over it. Add garlic, mustard, coriander, vinegar and jalapeño chillies. Mix well. Add oil in a thin stream beating continuously. Add water to get the right consistency. Ensure that the dressing does not get too runny. Cover and chill until ready to use.

To serve
Pour the dressing in a serving bowl and add the salad ingredients. With a salad fork and spoon, toss the salad gently. Season the salad with salt, pepper and cumin. Garnish with avocado slices and a sprig of coriander. Serve at once.

Serves } 4-6

Red Salsa (recipe on page 135)

Rosted Tomato Salsa (recipe on page 137)

Habanero Salsa (recipe on page 136)

Mango Salsa (recipe on page 136)

Taco Salad

Ingredients

2 cups taco chips

1 tsp taco seasoning

100 gm kidney beans

100 gm black beans

100 gm chickpeas

1 medium onion, finely chopped

1 cup finely-chopped red, yellow and green capsicum

½ cup finely-chopped spring onion

½ cup yellow corn kernels, boiled

2-3 tomatoes, deseeded and chopped

1 avocado, peeled and cubed

Juice of 1 lemon

Salt to taste

2 tbsp finely-chopped coriander leaves

3-4 finely-chopped jalapeño chillies

½ cup grated Cheddar cheese

To garnish
A few lettuce leaves

Method

Soak the beans and chickpeas overnight; boil and drain.

Mix cooked beans, chickpeas, onion, capsicum, spring onion, corn, tomatoes, avocado, taco seasoning, lemon juice, salt, coriander and jalapeño chillies. Toss gently to mix. Chill for an hour.

Just before serving, line a dish with lettuce leaves, spoon in the bean mixture and sprinkle grated cheese. Serve immediately with taco chips sprinkled around the salad plate.

Serves } 6-8

Ensalada con Almendras

(Salad Greens with Almonds)

Ingredients

3-4 cups mixed salad greens

¼ cup (each) dried cranberries, caramelized almonds and feta cheese or goat cheese

2 medium tomatoes, cubed

1 medium avocado, thinly sliced

1 medium red pepper, thinly sliced

For the dressing

¼ cup olive oil

2 tsp (each) balsamic and cider vinegar

½ tsp (each) salt, crushed red pepper, oregano and black pepper

To garnish

Fresh herbs

To serve

Taco basket

Method

Place vegetables in a bowl and chill. Place all the ingredients for the dressing in a jar and shake the jar to mix. Just before serving, toss the salad with the dressing, dried fruit, almonds, cheese and transfer onto taco basket. Garnish with fresh herbs and serve.

Note: To make taco basket, place rolled tortilla on the back of deep mould and press it down lightly. Deep-fry in hot oil until crisp. Allow the basket to cool slightly. Remove from mould with the help of a knife. Allow it to cool and store in an airtight box.

Serves } 6

Corn, Jalapeño and Cheese Mousse

Ingredients

2½ cups fresh corn kernels

1 tbsp whole milk

1 tsp gelatine

2-3 tbsp finely-chopped jalapeño chillies

¼ cup cream cheese spread

⅓ cup whipping cream

Salt and pepper to taste

To garnish

1-2 ears of corn, sliced jalapeños and sprigs of basil

To serve

Tortilla chips and Tomato Salad (recipe follows)

Method

Mix together milk and gelatine in a small bowl to soften.

Boil corn in a pan of boiling water until soft. Towel dry the corn and place in a food processor and process until very smooth. Press this warm corn through a sieve in a sauce pan. Add milk-gelatine mixture and cook on medium heat for 1 minute. Remove from fire and cool to room temperature.

Beat the cream in another bowl until it forms stiff peaks. Fold into corn mixture along with chopped jalapeños and cheese. Adjust the seasoning. Pour into mould or a glass bowl and chill until firm, at least 4 hours.

Unmould on a plate if set in a mould.

Tomato Salad

Toss together 1 medium chopped tomato with 1 tbsp virgin olive oil, 1½ tsp red wine vinegar, salt and pepper.

Garnish the mousse with 1-2 ears of corn, sliced jalapeños and basil leaves. Serve chilled with tortilla chips and tomato salad.

Serves } 6

Asparagus Guacamole

Ingredients

250 gm fresh asparagus spears, ends trimmed and cut into 2-inch pieces

or

1 can (425 gm) tinned asparagus, drained and chopped into 2-inch pieces

2 tbsp chopped chives or spring onion leaves

1 tbsp finely-chopped jalapeño chillies

1 clove garlic, crushed with ¼ tsp salt

1 tsp cumin powder

3 tbsp thick yogurt

1 tbsp lemon juice

To garnish

Sliced jalapeño chillies or freshly chopped chives

To serve

Raw vegetable sticks (crudités) or tortilla chips

Method

If using fresh asparagus, cook in salted water for seven to eight minutes or until soft. Remove and place in a bowl of ice water. Remove when cooled completely and dry on a kitchen towel.

Place remaining ingredients in a food processor or blender along with asparagus and blend until smooth. Transfer to a serving bowl and cool in the refrigerator for two to three hours.

Garnish with jalapeño chillies or chives and serve with vegetable sticks or tortilla chips.

Makes approximately 2 cups

Taco Dip

Ingredients

1 recipe Refried Beans (Page 148)

1 cup Red Salsa (Page 135)

1 cup Sour Cream (Page 245)

2 tsp taco seasoning

½ head iceberg lettuce, washed, rinsed and chopped

2 medium tomatoes, chopped

1 medium onion, finely chopped

½ cup sliced black olives

1 cup grated Monterey Jack or Cheddar cheese

To serve

Taco chips

Method

Layer the refried beans in a nine-inch round glass dish.

In a small bowl, mix together the salsa, sour cream and taco seasoning. Spread the mixture over the beans. Arrange the lettuce, tomato, onion, olives and cheese in layers over this. Cover with cling film and chill for one to two hours.

Serve with taco chips.

Serves } 6-8

Grilled Tomato Salsa

Ingredients

450 gm tomatoes

1 jalapeño chilli

1 clove garlic

½ tsp salt

1 tbsp finely-chopped coriander leaves

1 tsp vinegar

1 onion, finely chopped

1 tbsp oil

Method

Place each tomato directly on an open flame and blister the skin, turning all sides. Toast the jalapeño as well.

Peel the tomatoes, cut the stem off the chilli and place together in a food processor or a blender with garlic, salt, coriander leaves, vinegar and onion.

In a small saucepan, heat the oil and cook the salsa until it thickens slightly, about ten minutes. Serve at room temperature.

Makes 1½ cups

Red Salsa

Ingredients

4 tomatoes cut into large pieces

1 onion, cut into large pieces

5-6 cloves of garlic

4 Kashmiri red chillies

1 tbsp chopped coriander leaves

2 tbsp chopped jalapeño chillies

1 tbsp vinegar

1 tsp taco seasoning

A large pinch of oregano

Salt to taste

Method

Process all the ingredients in a food processor but do not process to a fine purée. It should be chunky.

Makes ½ a cup

Habanero Salsa

Ingredients

6 large tomatoes, finely chopped

1 large onion, finely chopped

1 cup finely-chopped cilantro

3 cloves garlic, minced

4 pieces (2 tbsp) Habanero chillies, soaked and minced

2 tbsp vinegar or lemon juice

1 tbsp orange juice

1 tsp dried oregano

1 tbsp salt

Method

Mix all the ingredients together in a bowl and allow it to stand overnight or at least for 6 hours.

Makes 1½ cups

Mango Salsa

Ingredients

250 gm raw mango, peeled and finely chopped

1 medium (each) onion and roasted red capsicum, finely chopped

1 tbsp (each) finely-chopped jalapeño and lemon juice

2 tbsp freshly-chopped mint

Salt to taste

Method

Mix all the ingredients together in a bowl and allow it to stand overnight or at least for 6 hours.

Makes 1½ cups

Roasted Tomato Salsa

Ingredients

5 medium tomatoes, roasted and peeled

5 small tomatoes, roasted and peeled

3-4 jalapeño chillies, roasted

2 medium red capsicums, roasted and peeled

1 head garlic, roasted

1 tsp (each) taco seasoning mix, red chilli paste and sugar

¼ cup (each) finely-chopped cilantro and lemon juice

Salt to taste

Method

Chop all roasted vegetables finely. Press the pulp out of the garlic and mix it with the vegetables. Add the remaining ingredients and chill for 3-4 hours or overnight.

Makes 2 cups

Baked Corn Salsa

Ingredients

1 cup boiled corn kernels

2 (each) tomatoes and onions, finely chopped

2-3 cloves garlic, crushed

1 tbsp oil

1 tsp (each) taco seasoning, cumin powder, oregano and chilli powder

½ cup finely-chopped red or green capsicum

2-3 tbsp (each) finely-chopped jalapeño chilli and coriander leaves

2 (7-inch) tortillas brushed with butter and cut into strips

¼ cup grated cheese

Salt to taste

To serve
Taco chips

Method

Heat the oil in a small frying pan; fry garlic, onions and capsicum for 2 minutes. Remove from the stove and transfer to a bowl. Add the tomatoes, corn, jalapeño chilli and coriander along with all the spices and salt. Toss to mix.

Transfer this to a shallow baking dish. Cover the top with cheese and arrange tortilla strips over. Bake in an oven at 400°F/200°C/Gas Mark 6 for 8-10 minutes. Serve hot with taco chips.

Serves } 4-6

Spicy Jack Twists with Salsa Ranch Dip

Ingredients

12-15 twisted bread sticks

1 cup Red Salsa (Page 135)

½ cup ranch dressing

1 cup shredded Monterey Jack cheese

1 tsp taco seasoning

½ tsp salt

2 tbsp butter

Method

In a small bowl combine the salsa and ranch dressing. Cover and refrigerate till ready to use. In a small bowl, mix together the cheese, taco seasoning and salt. Set aside. In an oven tray, toss breadsticks and butter lightly. Bake in a hot oven at 400°F/200°C/Gas Mark 6 for five minutes. Remove from the oven and sprinkle the cheese mixture evenly over the bread sticks. Bake again for five to seven minutes. Remove from the oven and set aside to cool. Serve with the chilled dip.

Serves } 4

Mexican Bean and Vegetable Wrap

Ingredients

1 cup Refried Beans (Page 148)

1 cup mixed grilled vegetables

1 cup Red Salsa (Page 135)

1 cup grated Monterey Jack cheese

½ cup jalapeño chillies, chopped

2 tbsp taco seasoning

1 cup Sour Cream (Page 245)

8 six-inch flour tortillas

1 medium avocado, sliced

A few lettuce leaves, shredded

To serve

Red Salsa (Page 135) and Sour Cream (Page 245)

Method

In a medium saucepan, mix together the beans, grilled vegetables, salsa, grated cheese, jalapeño chillies and taco seasoning. Cook gently until all the ingredients are mixed well. Remove from heat and add sour cream. Mix well. Warm the tortillas and spread a quarter cup of this mixture evenly over each tortilla. Sprinkle with shredded lettuce and a few pieces of avocado. Roll tightly and cut each roll into two diagonally and serve at once with additional salsa and sour cream.

Serves } 8

Taquitos with Grilled Tomato Salsa

Ingredients

6 flour tortillas

150 gm feta cheese, crumbled

2 tsp finely-chopped jalapeño chillies

½ tsp salt

½ tsp taco seasoning

2-3 tbsp oil

To serve

Grilled Tomato Salsa (Page 135)

Method

In a bowl, mix together the cheese, chillies, salt and taco seasoning.

Heat tortillas lightly on a griddle to make them pliable. Spoon one-sixth of the mixture onto each tortilla and spread it in a straight line near one edge so that it does not spill while frying. Carefully roll each tortilla tightly into a cigar-like shape and secure firmly with a toothpick.

Heat the oil in a frying pan and fry three taquitos at a time, turning over till brown on all sides. Remove from oil and drain on paper towels. Remove toothpick, cut each taquito into three. Serve immediately with grilled tomato salsa.

Makes 18 servings

Mushroom and Caramelised Onion Quesadillas with Jalapeño Chilli Jam

Ingredients

For the tortillas

½ cup maize flour (corn meal)

½ cup plain flour

1 tbsp spinach purée

1 tbsp chopped jalapeño chillies

1 tbsp oil

A pinch of salt

A pinch of oregano

For the filling

4 tbsp oil

1 large onion, finely chopped

1 tsp sugar

250 gm mushrooms, washed and chopped

¾ cup grated Cheddar or Monterey Jack cheese

Salt pepper and mustard to taste

To serve

Jalapeño Chilli Jam (Page147), Sour Cream (Page 245) and Red Salsa (Page 135)

Method

For the tortillas

Make a soft dough with all the ingredients for the tortillas. Cover and set aside for half an hour. Roll out five-inch round tortillas and dry roast them on a griddle. Wrap them in a piece of muslin and set aside.

Makes 12 tortillas

For the filling

Heat two tbsp of oil and sauté onion until soft. Add sugar and cook for two-three minutes more to caramelize.

In the remaining oil, sauté mushrooms with a little salt until soft. Mix onions and mushrooms and set aside to cool.

Toss the cheese with salt, pepper and mustard. Mix it with cooled vegetables.

On each tortilla spread one tbsp of this mixture and sandwich it with the other tortilla. Seal the edges with a little water. Set aside.

In a frying pan, fry each quesadilla with a little oil on both sides. Cut each one in four pieces and serve hot with chilli jam, sour cream and salsa.

Nachos Supreme

Ingredients

1 recipe Nacho sauce (recipe follows)

1 recipe Refried Beans (Page148)

1 recipe Red Salsa (Page 135)

½ cup chopped jalapeño chillies

200 gm tortilla chips

For nacho sauce

250 gm nacho cheese

1 tbsp finely-chopped jalapeño chillies

1 cup milk

1 tsp Taco seasoning

2 tbsp Red Salsa (Page 135)

To serve

Sour Cream (Page 245)

Method

For nacho sauce

Mix all the ingredients in a saucepan and bring to a boil. Remove from heat and set aside to cool slightly.

Makes 2 cups

To assemble nachos

Line a 4 inch-wide shallow dish with tortilla chips. Pile up beans, salsa, sliced jalapeños and finally, the nacho sauce on top of the chips. Place under a hot grill for two minutes and serve immediately with sour cream.

Serves } 6

Chilli and Cheese Spirals

Ingredients

100 gm cream cheese spread, softened

1 cup grated Monterey Jack and Cheddar cheese

½ cup diced jalapeño chillies

½ cup chopped red capsicum

½ cup chopped olives

½ cup chopped spring onions

1 tsp taco seasoning

4 (eight-inch) flour tortillas

To serve
Red Salsa (Page 135)

Method

Combine cream cheese, grated cheese, jalapeño chillies, red capsicum, olives, spring onion and taco seasoning in a bowl. Spread half a cup of cheese mixture over each tortilla; roll up. Wrap each roll in plastic wrap and refrigerate for one hour. Remove the wrap and cut each one into four pieces. Serve with salsa.

Makes 16 servings

Tacos

Ingredients

12 round (3") Taco shells

1 recipe Red Salsa (Page 135)

1 recipe Refried Beans (Page 148)

1 cup grated Cheddar or Monterey Jack cheese

1 cup shredded lettuce

½ cup sliced jalapeño chillies

Method

If taco shells are purchased from the store, crisp them slightly in the oven.

To assemble
Assemble each taco just before serving. Place taco shell on a plate, spread with ¼ cup refried beans followed by salsa. Sprinkle with 1-2 tbsp grated cheese and garnish with shredded lettuce and sliced jalapeños. Serve immediately.

Serves } 6

Sun-dried Tomato and Caramelized Onion Quesadillas

Ingredients

For the tortillas

½ cup (each) maize flour and plain flour

1 tbsp (each) sun-dried tomato purée and oil

A pinch of salt, paprika and oregano

Warm water to bind the dough

For the filling

¼ cup Red Chilli Jam (Page 147)

½ cup caramelized onions

½ cup sun-dried tomatoes, soaked and chopped

2 tbsp basil leaves, finely chopped

¾ cup grated Cheddar or Monterey Jack cheese

¼ cup salad oil (for cooking)

Salt, pepper and mustard to taste

To serve

Sour Cream (Page 245) and Red Salsa (Page 135)

Method

For the tortillas

Make soft dough with all the ingredients given above for the tortillas. Cover and set aside for ½ an hour. Roll out 5" round tortillas and dry roast them on a griddle. Wrap them in a muslin cloth and set aside.

Makes 12 tortillas.

Toss together sun-dried tomato, caramelized onions, basil and cheese with salt, pepper and mustard in a bowl. Add red chilli jam and mix well. Spread 1-2 tbsp of this mixture on one tortilla and sandwich it with the other tortilla. Seal the edges with little water. Set aside. Repeat this process for the remaining tortillas.

In a frying pan, fry each quesadilla with little oil on both sides. Cut each one into 4 pieces and serve hot with sour cream and salsa.

Makes 6 quesadillas

Mexican Corn Soup (recipe on page 122)

Black Bean, Corn, Potato and Pepper Salad (recipe on page 128)

Taco (recipe on page 143)

Caesar Salad Tacos

Ingredients

8 cups Romaine and iceberg lettuce, washed and cut into square pieces

2 cups grated Cheddar cheese

1 medium avocado, peeled, pitted and diced

½ cup (each) boiled black beans and corn

¼ cup finely-chopped jalapeños

⅓ cup Garlic Mayonnaise (Page 244) and ¼ cup Red Salsa (Page 135)

12 pieces taco shells, warmed

2 medium tomatoes, finely chopped

Salt to taste

Method

Combine lettuce, 1 cup cheese, avocado, beans, corn and jalapeño chillies in a large bowl.

Combine mayonnaise and salsa in a small bowl; mix well. Pour this over the lettuce mixture, tossing well to coat. Fill each taco shell with the salad mixture; top it with the remaining cheese and tomatoes. Serve immediately.

Serves } 12

Caribbean Vegetable Rice
(recipe on page 152)

Mexican Tortilla Casserole
(recipe on page 155)

Chimichanga

Ingredients

1 tbsp oil

1 medium (each) onion and red capsicum, finely chopped

1 tbsp finely-chopped jalapeño chillies

2 cloves garlic, chopped

2 medium tomatoes, chopped

½ cup boiled sweet corn kernels

½ cup Refried Beans (Page 148)

4 tbsp (each) Red Salsa (Page 135) and grated Cheddar cheese

4 stems spring onions

4 large flour tortillas

Oil for frying

To garnish and serve

Shredded iceberg lettuce, Sour Cream (Page 245) and salsa

Method

Heat oil in a large pan and stir-fry onion and capsicum until soft. Stir in jalapeño, garlic, tomatoes and sweet corn. Cook for 3-4 minutes. Add beans, salsa, cheese and spring onions. Mix well and set aside to cool.

Warm a tortilla in a hot frying pan until soft and flexible. Place a quarter of the mixture onto the centre of the tortilla and fold over the edges to form a neat parcel. Pin in place with a toothpick and repeat with the remaining tortillas. Heat the oil in a frying pan and deep-fry the chimichanga for 2-3 minutes on each side until crisp and golden brown. Drain on paper towel, cut into 2 or 3 pieces and serve with shredded lettuce, sour cream and salsa.

Alternatively, place chimichanga on a greased baking dish and bake for 15 minutes in an oven at 400°F/200°C/Gas Mark 6.

Serves } 4

Red Chilli Jam

Ingredients

2 tbsp oil

1 tbsp ginger-garlic paste

½ cup finely-chopped dried red chillies

¼ cup sugar

A pinch of salt

2 tbsp vinegar

Method

Heat oil in a small saucepan; fry ginger-garlic paste for one minute. Add the chillies and cook for two to three minutes. Add sugar, salt and vinegar. Cook until sugar has melted and is of a syrupy consistency. Remove from heat and cool.

Makes ¾ cup

Jalapeño Chilli Jam

Ingredients

2 tbsp oil

1 inch piece ginger, finely chopped

3 cloves garlic, finely chopped

½ cup finely-chopped jalapeño chillies

¼ cup vinegar

¼ cup sugar

Method

Heat the oil in a saucepan and fry ginger and garlic for four to five minutes. Add the remaining ingredients and boil until thick. Set aside to cool and store in an airtight container in the refrigerator.

Makes ¾ cup

Refried Beans

Ingredients

200 gm kidney beans

1 onion, roughly chopped

2-3 cloves of garlic

Salt to taste

1 tbsp taco seasoning

2 tbsp Red Salsa (Page 135)

Method

Soak the beans overnight or for six to eight hours. Place in a pressure cooker with onion, garlic and salt. Cook for three to four whistles. Remove from heat and set aside to cool. Remove from pressure cooker and mash lightly; add taco seasoning and salsa. Use this mixture as taco or burrito filling or as an accompaniment to the enchiladas.

Makes 3 cups

Guacamole

Ingredients

1 ripe avocado

2-3 tbsp lemon juice

1 tbsp fresh coriander, chopped

2-3 chopped green chilies or jalapeño peppers

2 cloves garlic, mashed

2-3 tbsp minced onion

1 tomato, peeled, deseeded and chopped

1 tbsp mayonnaise

Salt to taste

Method

Cut and mash the avocado with a fork while blending in the lemon juice. Add salt, coriander, chillies, garlic, onion, tomato and mayonnaise. Mix thoroughly and chill. Serve chilled with tortilla chips.

Makes 1 cup

Enchilada Pie

Ingredients

1 cup Enchilada Sauce (recipe follows)

1 onion, finely chopped

2 cups Refried Beans (Page 148)

1 tsp salt

1 tsp taco seasoning

1 tsp chilli powder

6 six-inch Corn Tortillas (recipe follows)

Butter to grease the tortillas

½ cup sliced olives

½ cup finely-chopped spring onions

1½ cups grated sharp Cheddar cheese

1 tbsp butter

Method

In a wide frying pan brown onions and beans over a medium heat. Add salt, taco seasoning, chilli powder and enchilada sauce. Spread each tortilla with butter. In an 8"-round pie dish, arrange alternate layers of tortillas, beans, olives, spring onions and cheese. Add half a cup of water, cover and bake in an oven preheated to 400°F/200°C/Gas Mark 6 for twenty minutes. Cut into wedges and serve.

Serves } 4-6

Corn Tortillas
Make dough with 1 cup of maize flour (corn meal), 1 tbsp plain flour, a pinch of salt and ⅔ cup of warm water. Divide into 6 equal parts and roll into 6-inch tortillas. Roast on a hot griddle on both sides, till brown specks appear.

Makes 6 tortillas

Enchilada Sauce

Ingredients

4 tbsp sliced jalapeño chillies

1 clove garlic, minced

¼ cup tomato purée

1 tsp oregano

¼ tsp cumin powder

3 tbsp salad oil

1½ tsp salt

Method

Roast the jalapeños in a hot oven for three to four minutes and set aside to cool. Make a smooth paste with a little water; set aside. Heat oil in a saucepan; fry garlic and jalapeño paste for one minute. Add the remaining ingredients and 1½ cups of water. Simmer for ten minutes.

Makes 1½ cups

Corn and Cheese Enchiladas

Ingredients

For the enchiladas

2 cups fresh corn kernels, boiled

1 cup grated cheese

½ cup finely-chopped green onions

Salt and pepper to taste

Taco seasoning and mustard to taste

6 seven-inch round tortillas

½ cup Red Salsa (Page 135)

Oil to fry the tortillas

For the sauce

2 cups Vegetable Stock (Page 245)

3 tbsp plain flour

4 tbsp oil

1 medium onion, finely chopped

2 cloves garlic, chopped

2 large tomatoes, blanched and chopped

3 tbsp finely-chopped jalapeño chillies

½ tsp cumin powder

½ tsp salt

Method

For the sauce
In a bowl, mix together the stock and flour. Heat oil in a saucepan; fry the onion and garlic until soft. Add the tomatoes, chillies, cumin and salt. Cook for two to three minutes. Add the stock and flour mixture.

Stirring continuously bring to a boil. Simmer for five to ten minutes until the sauce thickens. Remove from heat and set aside.

For the enchiladas
Mix together corn, cheese, green onions, salt, pepper, taco seasoning and mustard. Toss gently to mix and set aside.

Heat one tsp oil in a frying pan; fry one tortilla at a time. Spread a little salsa on the top of each tortilla, turn over and spread a little more salsa on the other side and let it sizzle a bit. Remove from the frying pan and place it on a board. Spread two to three tbsp of the corn mixture in the centre vertically. Fold in both sides of the tortilla, so they overlap slightly. Place on a greased baking dish. Repeat the same for the rest of the tortillas.

If not using immediately, cover with cling film and refrigerate. When ready to serve, remove from the refrigerator, spoon the sauce over the tortillas, sprinkle a little cheese and bake in an oven at 400°F/200°C/Gas Mark 6 for eight to ten minutes. Serve immediately.

Serves | 6

Layered Mexican Rice

Ingredients

For the rice

2 cups long grain rice
1 tbsp olive oil
1½ tsp salt
Salt and pepper to taste

For the red layer

3-4 cloves garlic
1 tbsp coriander leaves
½ tsp salt
1 tbsp vinegar
1 tsp taco seasoning
A pinch of oregano
2 cups tomatoes
1 onion
1 tbsp olive oil
1 cup finely-chopped red capsicum
½ cup finely-chopped onion
½ cup kidney beans, boiled

For the green layer

2 tbsp olive oil
1½ cups finely-chopped green capsicum
¾ cup finely-chopped onion
½ cup finely-chopped fresh basil
½ cup grated Cheddar cheese
½ cup black beans, boiled

For the sour cream layer

2 cloves garlic, crushed
1 tbsp finely-chopped chives
1 cup thick yogurt
1 tbsp lemon juice
½ cup fresh cream

To garnish

Sliced jalapeños and basil leaves

Method

For the rice

Combine five and-a-half cups of water, olive oil and salt in a large saucepan. Bring to a boil and add the rice. Cover and cook until liquid is absorbed and rice is tender yet firm, approximately twenty minutes. Fluff up the rice with a fork. Spread out on a baking sheet and cool completely. Season with salt and pepper to taste. Divide the rice into two portions; one for the red layer and one for the green.

For the red layer

Blend together the garlic, coriander, salt, vinegar, taco seasoning, oregano, tomatoes and onion in a food processor to make a salsa sauce. Heat oil in a small frying pan and fry red capsicum and beans for a short time. Remove from heat and transfer to a bowl. Add the salsa and mix well. Toss one portion of rice with the mixture and arrange in a baking dish. Set aside.

For the green layer

Heat oil in a small frying pan and fry the green capsicum and onion until slightly soft. Add the basil, take it off the heat, and mix with the other portion of the rice. Adjust salt and layer over the red layer. Sprinkle cheese all over and bake in an oven at 400°F/200°C/ Gas Mark 6 for fifteen minutes. Remove from the oven, spread sour cream evenly on top, garnish with jalapeños and basil and serve immediately.

For the sour cream layer

Mix all the ingredients together and keep chilled until required.

Serves } 8-10

Caribbean Vegetable Rice

Ingredients

For the rice

1½ cups long grain rice, washed and soaked

2 cups Vegetable Stock (Page 245)

2 tbsp oil

1 tbsp red chilli paste

1 clove garlic, crushed

½ cup tomato purée

Salt to taste

For the vegetables

2 tbsp oil

1 onion, finely chopped

1 medium red capsicum

1 tbsp chilli paste

5-6 small tomatoes, deseeded and chopped

2 cups mixed boiled vegetables (zucchini, peas, carrots, beans)

1 tsp salt

1 tsp taco seasoning

1 tbsp butter

1 tbsp plain flour

1 cup thick coconut milk

To garnish

Finely-chopped parsley and chilli flakes

Method

For the rice

Cook the rice briskly in vegetable stock until just tender. In a wide pan, heat oil and fry chilli paste and garlic for one minute. Add the rice, tomato purée and salt; toss gently. Transfer rice to a greased baking dish and keep warm.

For the vegetables

Heat oil in a frying pan; fry onion, red capsicum and chilli paste for three to four minutes. Add the tomatoes, vegetables, salt and taco seasoning.

In a small pan melt the butter; add flour and cook for a few seconds. Add coconut milk gradually and cook stirring continuously, until thick. Remove from heat and add to the vegetable mixture. Simmer for two to three minutes. Pour the mixture over rice, garnish with parsley and chilli flakes, and serve hot.

Serves } 6

Creole Rice

Ingredients

1 cup long grain rice, washed and soaked in water

2 cups Vegetable Stock (Page 245)

1 tbsp olive oil

1 tbsp butter

1 medium onion, chopped

2-3 cloves garlic, crushed

1 medium green capsicum, chopped

1 medium red capsicum, chopped

¼ cup white or black beans, soaked overnight and boiled

For tomato sauce

500 gm tomatoes, blanched and coarsely chopped

2 tbsp chopped jalapeño chillies

1 tsp chopped parsley

1 tsp chopped dried oregano

1 tbsp butter

½ tsp salt

½ tsp pepper powder

To garnish

¼ cup grated cheese

1 tsp red chilli flakes

¼ cup chopped coriander leaves

¼ cup spring onions

Method

Boil the vegetable stock and add soaked rice. Cook briskly until just tender. Remove from heat and set aside. Heat the oil and butter together in a wide pan. Add onion and garlic and cook until soft. Add capsicums and beans and cook for two more minutes. Add cooked rice, mix well and set aside.

In another saucepan, mix all the ingredients for the tomato sauce and bring to a boil. Add to the rice mixture and toss gently. Pour into a baking dish. Sprinkle with cheese and chilli flakes. Just before serving, bake in an oven at 400°F/200°C/Gas Mark 6 for ten minutes. Garnish with spring onions and coriander and serve.

Serves } 4–6

Tex-Mex Quiche

Ingredients

1 nine-inch round pie crust

2 tbsp olive oil

4 tbsp butter

¼ cup finely-chopped mushrooms

¼ cup finely-chopped red capsicum

¼ cup finely-chopped green capsicum

¼ cup finely-chopped white onions

2 tbsp garlic

¼ cup finely-chopped tomatoes

¾ cup cream cheese

⅔ cup milk

1 tbsp cornflour

1 tbsp plain flour

¼ cup finely-chopped spring onions

2 tbsp finely-chopped jalapeño chillies

¾ cup grated Cheddar cheese

¾ cup grated Monterey Jack cheese

1 tbsp chilli powder

1 tbsp taco seasoning

1 tbsp salt

¾ cup Refried Beans (Page 148), partially mashed

To serve

Sour Cream (Page 245), Red Salsa (Page 135)

Method

In a small frying pan, heat the olive oil and two tbsp of butter. Add mushrooms, capsicum, white onion and garlic. Cook until mushrooms change colour. Add the tomatoes and cook for two more minutes. Remove from heat and set aside to cool.

In a large bowl, mix together cream cheese, milk and both kinds of flour. Beat until smooth. Add spring onions, jalapeño chillies, grated cheese and all the spices and salt. Add refried beans and mix again. Add the sautéed mushrooms, capsicum, onion and garlic. Stir until all the vegetables are well-coated with the sauce.

With a large spoon fill the pie shell with this mixture. Cut the remaining two tbsp of butter into small cubes and place them on top of the pie at random. Bake in an oven at 350°F/180°C/Gas Mark 4 for twenty-five to thirty minutes, or until the top of the pie just starts to turn brown. Remove from the oven and cool slightly. Serve warm or at room temperature with salsa and sour cream.

Serves } 6

Mexican Tortilla Casserole

Ingredients

1 cup milk mixed with 1 tbsp maize flour

Salt to taste

Pepper to taste

Taco seasoning to taste

1 cup mixed boiled vegetables (zucchini, corn, peas, carrots, French beans etc.)

1 recipe Refried Beans (Page 148)

½ cup Red Salsa (Page 135)

½ cup sliced jalapeños

½ cup sliced olives

½ cup finely-chopped spring onions

1 tbsp butter

To garnish

1 cup crushed tortilla chips, parsley and chilli flakes

Method

Grease an 8"x8" baking dish with butter. Spread refried beans evenly at the bottom of the dish. Boil the milk and maize flour mixture on medium heat until thick. Add salt, pepper, taco seasoning and boiled vegetables. Cook for four to five minutes. Remove from heat and leave to cool slightly.

Spread the vegetable mixture over the bean mixture. Spread salsa, jalapeños, olives and spring onions over the vegetables. Sprinkle grated cheese and bake in an oven at 400°F/200°C/Gas Mark 6 for twelve to fifteen minutes. Remove and sprinkle tortilla chips and garnish with parsley and chilli flakes. Serve hot.

Serves } 6

Tex-Mex Cornbread

Ingredients

1 cup maize flour

¾ cup plain flour, sieved

2 tbsp sugar

¾ tsp (each) salt and baking soda

1 tbsp baking powder

1 cup milk

¼ cup cream

3 tbsp vegetable oil

2 tbsp (each) finely-chopped jalapeño chilli and red capsicum

¾ cup corn niblets

2 tbsp melted butter

Greased 13 x 9 x 2 inch baking pan

To serve

Sour cream (Page 245)

Red Chilli Jam (Page 147)

Method

Preheat the oven to 350°F/180°C/Gas Mark 4. In a large bowl mix together maize flour, plain flour, sugar, salt, baking soda and baking powder. Add the remaining ingredients and mix well. Pour this mixture into greased tin. Bake the bread in a preheated oven for 30 minutes or until top is golden.

Remove from oven, brush the bread with melted butter and set aside to cool. Cut into square pieces and serve with sour cream and chilli jam.

Serves } 8

Sizzling Vegetable Fajitas

Ingredients

2 cups mixed vegetables (zucchini, baby corn, carrots, French beans and spring onion), cut into strips

1 medium (each) red and green capsicums and onion, cut into strips

2 tbsp (each) olive oil and melted butter

6-8 (6-inch) flour tortillas

For marinade

2 tbsp olive oil

1 tsp (each) crushed red chilli flakes, cumin powder, pepper, dried oregano and salt

6 cloves crushed garlic

1 tbsp (each) brown sugar, wine vinegar and chopped cilantro

¼ cup water

Juice and grated rind of 1 lemon

To serve

Red Salsa (Page 135), Sour Cream (Page 245), grated cheese and Guacamole (Page 148)

Iron plate to serve the vegetables and a basket to keep tortillas warm

Method

Mix all the ingredients for the marinade in a blender jar and blend until smooth. Place mixed vegetables in a bowl and pour the marinade mixture over, toss gently and set aside for 30 minutes.

Heat oil in a large frying pan and cook the marinated vegetables for 3-4 minutes. Add capsicums and onion and cook for a further 3-4 minutes or until vegetables are tender yet crisp.

Heat the iron plate ten minutes before serving in a hot oven. Grease the plate with a little oil; place it on the wooden base. Transfer hot vegetable mixture onto the plate. Bring the plate to the table and drizzle melted butter all around the vegetable mixture to make a sizzling sound. Serve with warmed tortillas in a basket along with salsa, sour cream, grated cheese and guacamole. To serve, spread a little salsa over a warm tortilla, top it with guacamole. Heap a tbsp of vegetable mixture in the centre and finish with dollop of sour cream. Fold tortilla over the filling and serve right away.

Serves } 6

Fiesta Corn Skillet

Ingredients

1 medium (each) onion and capsicum, chopped into small cubes

1 tin (330 gm) yellow corn kernels, drained

1 cup (each) Refried Beans (Page 148) and mixed boiled vegetables

2 tbsp taco seasoning mix

1 cup grated Cheddar cheese

¾ cup maize flour, sieved

¼ cup plain flour

2 tsp (each) powdered sugar, baking powder and oregano

¾ tsp (each) salt and baking soda

½ cup (each) thick milk and cream

Butter to grease the skillet and to brush on top

To garnish

Freshly-chopped herbs and Sour Cream (Page 245)

Method

Grease an iron skillet with butter. Place it on the stove and toss onion and capsicum lightly. Add corn, vegetables, refried beans, taco seasoning mix and cheese. Mix well. Remove from stove and set aside.

In a small bowl mix the two types of flour, sugar, baking powder, oregano, salt and soda. Mix milk and cream together and add to the flour mixture. Stir until just blended. Spread this over bean-vegetable mixture. Smoothen the surface and brush the top with butter.

Bake in hot oven at 350°F/180°C/Gas Mark 4 for 20-25 minutes or until wooden toothpick comes out clean. Garnish with fresh herbs and dollops of sour cream.

Serves } 6

Pan Asian

The cuisine of Asia is mind-boggling in its variety, to say the least. Pan Asian cuisine uses traditional and unique spices and condiments like galangal, lemon grass, tofu and ajinomoto. So get set for some superb fare like Korean Kimchi, Malaysian Chilli Noodles, Vegetable Sui Mai, Thai Vegetable Cakes and those eternal favourites– Vegetable Spring Rolls and Wonton Soup!

Hot and Sour Vegetable Soup

Ingredients

¼ cup shredded cabbage

¼ cup shredded carrots

¼ cup French beans cut into thin strips

¼ cup chopped cauliflower

¼ cup green capsicum, cut into thin strips

2 tbsp oil

A pinch of MSG (optional)

5 tbsp cornflour mixed with 1 cup water

1 tsp black pepper powder

1 tsp soy sauce

¾ tsp chilli sauce

2 tbsp vinegar

½ tsp sugar

Salt to taste

¼ cup bean curd, cut into 2-inch long strips

5 cups water or Clear Vegetable Stock (Page 165)

2 eggs, beaten (optional)

To garnish

Finely chopped coriander leaves

Method

Heat oil in a saucepan; add the vegetables, bean curd and MSG. Stir-fry on high heat for two minutes. Add water or the stock, cornflour mixture, pepper, soy sauce, chilli sauce, vinegar, sugar and salt. Bring to a boil, stirring continuously and simmer for one minute. Add the bean curd strips.

Garnish with coriander leaves and serve hot.

Serves } 4

Note: If you wish to add eggs to this soup, lightly beat two eggs and pour it in a thin stream into the boiling soup; stir briskly till the egg separates into shreds. Turn off heat and do not boil the soup thereafter. Garnish and serve.

Water Chestnut and Mango Salad (recipe on page 167)

Malay Curry (recipe on page 194)

Roti Canai (recipe on page 194)

Oriental Vegetables with Peanut Sauce (recipe on page 175)

Wonton Soup

Ingredients

For the wontons

18 wonton wrappers

1 tbsp oil

½ cup mixed vegetables, (such as cabbage, carrot and French beans), finely chopped

¼ cup finely-chopped spring onions

A pinch of MSG (optional)

½ tsp salt

½ tsp sugar

½ tsp pepper powder

1 tsp soy sauce

For the soup

6 cups water or Clear Vegetable Stock (Page 165)

¼ cup finely-chopped spring onions

¼ cup finely-chopped carrots

¼ cup finely-chopped capsicum

Salt to taste

1 tsp pepper powder

1 tbsp crushed ginger

1 tsp sugar

1 tbsp soy sauce

To serve

Chilli sauce

Method

For the wontons

Heat oil in a frying pan; stir-fry the vegetables and spring onions and add the MSG if using. Add salt, sugar, pepper and soy sauce. Remove from heat and set aside to cool.

Put one tsp of the filling in the centre of each wonton wrapper, moisten one side and fold the other side over to form a triangle. Take two opposite ends of the triangle and moisten the corners of both and stick them together to form a wonton shape. Set aside on the floured surface to dry. Repeat this process for the rest of the wrappers.

Cook wontons in boiling salted water for five to seven minutes, drain and set aside.

For the soup

Bring the vegetable stock or water to a boil. Add the vegetables, salt, pepper, ginger, soy sauce and sugar. Just before serving, add the wontons and serve hot with chilli sauce. Allow three wontons per serving.

Serves } 6

Massaman Curry
(recipe on page 192)

Vegetable Sui Mai
(recipe on page 177)

Sweet Corn Vegetable Soup
(recipe on page 165)

Lemon and Coriander Soup

Ingredients

1 tsp lemon juice

1 tbsp coriander leaves, finely chopped

6 cups Clear Vegetable Stock (Page 165) or water

2 tsp oil

2 cups mixed vegetables such as cauliflower, mushrooms, carrots and capsicums, cut into cubes

2 stalks spring onions cut lengthways

A pinch of MSG (optional)

Salt to taste

1 green chilli, slit

3-4 stalks lemon grass

Method

Bring the stock to a boil, lower heat and simmer. Heat oil in a saucepan; stir-fry the vegetables along with spring onions. Add MSG and cook over high heat for three to four minutes. Add salt, green chilli, lemon grass and the simmering stock. Bring to a boil. Add lemon juice and coriander just before serving.

Serves } 6

Mongolian Hot Pot

This is a popular dish in China and Mongolia, served at reunion dinners, where everyone sits around a table and cooks their portion of food in a simmering hot pot.

Ingredients

For the stock

1 carrot

1 onion

4-5 black peppercorns

1 inch ginger

1 stalk spring onion

1 stick celery

6 cups water

For dips and garnishes

2 cups Chinese cabbage leaves, coarsely chopped

200 gm tofu (bean curd), cubed

100 gm rice noodles, soaked in hot water

2-3 tbsp sesame paste

¼ cup soy sauce mixed with ¼ cup water

¼ cup rice vinegar

¼ cup chilli oil

¼ cup finely chopped coriander

4 tbsp chopped garlic, soaked in a little vinegar and salt

Method

For the stock

Heat the stock ingredients in a pot, and simmer for thirty minutes. Strain and transfer the stock to a ceramic or metal dish, which can be heated over a burner at the table. Bring it back to a boil.

Arrange all the garnishes and dips in individual bowls and place them on the table. Diners make up their own portion of the vegetables and bean curd, seasoning them to taste with dips and sauces. Noodles are placed in each bowl and topped with simmering stock, to which sauces have been added. This soup is eaten as a final course.

Serves } 6

Laksa Lemak

Spicy Noodle soup

Ingredients

For the soup

200 gm thin noodles

3-4 tbsp oil

1 inch ginger, thinly sliced

4 cups Clear Vegetable Stock (Page 165) or water

2 cups thin coconut milk

1 tbsp sugar

Salt to taste

100 gm bean curd or tofu, shredded

1 cup bean sprouts, blanched

1 cup chopped mushrooms

1 tbsp finely-chopped basil leaves

4 stalks spring onions, chopped

For the spice paste

8 dried red chillies, soaked and chopped

10 shallots, chopped

1 stalk lemon grass, chopped

¾ inch galangal, chopped

¼ inch fresh turmeric, chopped

3-4 cloves garlic

1 tbsp oil

To garnish

Sliced red chillies, sliced lemon and spring onions

Method

To make the spice paste, process all the ingredients in a blender to a fine paste. Heat oil for the soup and fry the paste for seven to eight minutes. Add ginger and stock and bring to a boil. Add coconut milk, sugar and salt. Reduce heat and simmer for 3-5 minutes. Plunge noodles in boiling water for a few seconds to heat through.

To serve, divide the bean curd, bean sprouts and mushrooms among six soup bowls. Top with basil leaves and pour the soup over; add spring onions and chillies. Serve with lemon slices on the side.

Serves } 6

Sweet Corn Vegetable Soup

Ingredients

1 cup tinned cream-style corn

¾ cup shredded boiled vegetables (carrots, beans and cauliflower)

5 cups water

Salt to taste

1 tsp pepper

1 tsp sugar

1 tsp soy sauce

¼ tsp MSG (optional)

5 tbsp cornflour, mixed with 1 cup water

To Serve

Green chillies in vinegar

Method

Boil the water and add the corn, salt, pepper, sugar, soy sauce and MSG. Stir and simmer, uncovered for three-four minutes.

Add the boiled vegetables. Raise the heat and add the cornflour mixture, stirring all the time, until the soup thickens. Simmer for one minute.

Serve hot with chillies in vinegar.

Serves } 4

Clear Vegetable Stock

Ingredients

2 medium onions, chopped

1 carrot, chopped

½ cup roughly-chopped cabbage,

5-6 stalks celery, chopped

½ cup roughly-chopped spring onion

5-6 French beans, chopped

1 inch piece ginger

6½ cups water

½ tsp salt

Method

Mix all the ingredients and pressure cook for ten to fifteen minutes. Leave to cool and strain. Use the strained liquid as stock. Do not purée or liquidize the vegetables.

Makes 6 cups

Gado Gado

Indonesian Salad

Ingredients

For the salad

100 gm bean sprouts

100 gm snow peas

100 gm tomatoes

100 gm French beans

100 gm broccoli

100 gm carrots

100 gm potatoes

100 gm bean curd

100 gm cauliflower

3 large eggs, boiled and cut lengthways (optional)

A few lettuce leaves to line the plate

For the peanut sauce

1 1/3 cup roasted peanuts

½ cup sesame oil

6-8 bird's eye chillies

2 cloves garlic

4-5 shallots

2 tbsp brown sugar

1 tbsp soy sauce

2 cups water

1 tbsp tamarind water or juice of 1 lemon

Salt to taste

To garnish

Fried onions, peanuts and coconut slices

Method

For the salad

Cut snow peas and French beans diagonally into one-inch pieces, cauliflower and broccoli into florets, potatoes and tomatoes into wedges, carrots and bean curd into two-inch lengths. Blanch or boil each vegetable separately. Keep warm.

For the peanut sauce

Fry the peanuts in oil till slightly brown. Drain, cool, pound coarsely and set aside. Crush bird's eye chillies, garlic and shallots together and fry in the same oil. Add the rest of the ingredients along with peanuts and cook until the sauce is thick. Cool slightly.

To serve the salad, pile the vegetables in the centre of a serving plate, which is lined with lettuce, arrange the egg slices on top (if using) and pour the sauce over. Garnish with onions, peanuts and coconut slices. Serve immediately.

Serves } 6–8

Water Chestnut and Mango Salad

Ingredients

1 ½ cups shelled water chestnuts

½ cup finely shredded unripe green mango

½ tsp soy sauce

Salt to taste

Sugar to taste

2-3 fresh red chillies finely chopped

To garnish

Finely-chopped coriander

Method

Cut the water chestnuts in half and wash in cold water. Drain and set aside.

Place grated mango in a serving bowl; add water chestnuts, soy sauce, salt, sugar and chillies. Toss gently to mix.

Garnish with coriander and chill until ready to serve.

Serves } 4

Thai Noodle Salad

Ingredients

For the salad

200 gm rice noodles

1 cup shredded cabbage, washed and drained

1 medium carrot thinly cut

1 bunch spring onions, sliced

½ medium red capsicum sliced thinly

½ medium yellow capsicum sliced thinly

½ cup roasted and coarsely ground peanuts

For the dressing

2 tbsp sesame oil

1 tbsp finely chopped garlic

1 tbsp chopped red chilli

¼ cup Clear Vegetable Stock (Page 165)

2 tbsp rice vinegar

1 tbsp raw brown sugar

1 tbsp lemon juice

1 tbsp soy sauce

½ tsp pepper powder

Salt to taste

To garnish

Finely chopped coriander, fresh red chillies and celery leaves

Method

Boil the noodles according to the instructions on the packet. Mix vegetables with the noodles, place in a bowl and chill until ready to serve.

For the dressing
Heat oil in a saucepan; add garlic and chilli and fry for a few seconds. Add the stock followed by the rest of the ingredients and remove from heat. Set aside to cool.

Just before serving, sprinkle peanuts and drizzle the dressing over the chilled salad. Garnish with coriander, red chillies and celery leaves.

Serves } 6

Crispy Rice Cakes with Coconut-mushroom Sauce

Ingredients

For crispy rice cakes

2½ cups cold, boiled rice

Oil for deep-frying

For the sauce

1 tsp chopped garlic

1 tsp chopped coriander roots

1 tsp black peppercorns

1 tbsp finely-chopped shallots

1/3 cup finely chopped mushrooms

1 cup thick coconut milk

1 tbsp tamarind juice

1 tbsp soy sauce

2 tbsp lemon juice

2 tbsp powdered peanuts

1 large red chilli, finely chopped

2 tbsp oil

1 tsp sugar

To garnish

Coriander leaves

Method

For crispy rice cakes

Take a ball of cold rice (approximately two tbsp) and press between your palms to form a pancake, about a quarter inch thick.

Deep-fry the cakes in hot oil until golden brown and crisp. Drain and store in an airtight container.

For the sauce

In a mortar, pound together garlic, coriander roots and peppercorns to a paste.

Heat oil in a pan and fry the paste for a few minutes. Add the shallots and mushrooms and stir. Add coconut milk and all the remaining ingredients and mix thoroughly.

Transfer to a serving bowl, garnish with coriander leaves and serve with rice cakes.

Serves } 4–6

Vegetable Spring Rolls

Ingredients

12-15 spring roll wrappers

For the filling

1 carrot, shredded

½ cup shredded cabbage

½ cup shredded capsicum

½ cup bean sprouts, roughly chopped

6-8 French beans, chopped

2 tbsp oil

1 onion, finely chopped

Salt to taste

½ tsp pepper

½ tsp sugar

½ tsp MSG (optional)

½ cup noodles, boiled

1 tsp soy sauce

2 tsp cornflour mixed with ¼ cup water

Oil for frying

To serve

Chilli sauce

Method

For the filling

Heat the oil in a pan and fry the onion and vegetables for one minute. Add salt, pepper, sugar and MSG. Chop the noodles roughly and add them to the vegetable mixture along with soy sauce. Mix well. Remove from heat and set aside to cool.

Cut each spring roll wrapper into a square of the required size. Place one tbsp of the vegetable mixture in the centre. Brush all four edges with cornflour paste and roll the wrapper into a cylindrical shape. Seal the edges.

When ready to serve, deep-fry the rolls in hot oil until crisp. Serve at once with chilli sauce.

Serves } 4-6

Spring Onion Pancakes

Ingredients

For the pancakes

½ cup plain flour

½ cup water

¼ tsp salt

1 egg

¼ tsp baking powder

1 tbsp oil + for deep-frying

1 tbsp cornflour

1 tbsp water

For the filling

3 cups finely-chopped spring onions

A pinch of MSG (optional)

½ tsp salt

½ tsp pepper

½ tsp sugar

½ tsp soy sauce

To serve

Soy-chilli sauce

Method

For the pancakes

Sift the flour and the baking powder into a bowl. Add the rest of the ingredients and mix well. Heat a non-stick pan and grease with a little oil. Pour three tbsp of batter at a time and cook each pancake on both sides, remove and set aside. Repeat with the remaining pancakes. This will give you ten, six to seven-inch round pancakes.

For the filling

Heat oil in a frying pan; add spring onions and MSG. Cook over high heat for two minutes. Add salt, pepper, sugar and soy sauce. Cook till the mixture is dry. Set aside to cool.

To assemble the pancakes, place each pancake on a board or flat surface and spread two to three tbsp of the onion mixture. Make a paste with cornflour and one tbsp of water. Apply the cornflour paste around the edges. Fold the pancake in a cylindrical shape, flatten it slightly and seal the edges. Deep-fry in oil. Drain on kitchen paper, cut each pancake into three pieces and serve hot with soy-chilli sauce.

Serves } 6-8

Chilli Bean Curd

Ingredients

1 tbsp plain flour

1 tbsp cornflour

½ tsp salt

200 gm bean curd, cut into 1-inch pieces

2 tbsp oil + for frying

2 tsp butter

4-5 green chillies, slit lengthways

1 tbsp crushed ginger

4-5 cloves garlic, crushed

½ tsp salt

½ tsp pepper powder

½ tsp sugar

A pinch of MSG (optional)

2 tsp soy sauce

1 tbsp chilli sauce

½ tbsp vinegar

2 stalks spring onion, cut lengthways

1 tbsp finely-chopped coriander leaves

Note: You may use pieces of cottage cheese or vegetables like baby corn and mushrooms in place of bean curd.

Method

Mix together plain flour, cornflour and salt. Roll bean curd in the mixture and fry in batches in hot oil till golden brown. Set aside.

In a separate frying pan, heat butter and two tsp oil together and fry green chillies, ginger, and garlic. Add salt, pepper, sugar and MSG. Add soy sauce, chilli sauce and vinegar and stir. Add a little water to prevent the mixture from sticking to the pan. Add bean curd, spring onions and coriander and mix well.

Serve hot on toothpicks.

Serves } 4

Sesame Corn on Toast

Ingredients

1 tbsp sesame seeds

150 gm cream-style corn

2 finely-chopped green chillies

1 tbsp cornflour

1 tsp soy sauce

Salt to taste

A pinch of MSG (optional)

6 slices white bread

3 tbsp plain flour

Oil for deep-frying

To serve
Chilli sauce

Method

Mix together the corn, chillies, cornflour, soy sauce, salt and MSG.

Make a paste with the flour and three tbsp water.

Remove the crust from the bread slices and cut each one into four squares. Spread one tbsp of corn mixture on each square, pressing down well. Spread a little of the flour paste on it and sprinkle with some sesame seeds. Deep-fry the bread squares in hot oil until golden brown. Drain on absorbent paper and serve hot with chilli sauce.

Serves } 6

Thai Vegetable Cakes

Ingredients

For the cakes

½ cup (each) mashed potatoes and crumbled tofu

1 cup finely-chopped vegetables (babycorn, beans, water chestnuts, spring onions etc)

2 tbsp (each) finely-chopped coriander root, lime leaves and basil

1-2 tbsp green Thai curry paste

1 tsp (each) soy sauce and sugar

Salt to taste

¼ cup plain flour mixed with little water

½ cup breadcrumbs or vermicelli (to coat)

Oil for shallow-frying

To garnish

Crisp fried basil and coriander leaves

To serve

Tomato-Chilli Jam (recipe follows)

For tomato-chilli jam

6 medium tomatoes, blanched and roughly chopped

6 pieces dried red chillies, deseeded, chopped and soaked

2 cloves garlic, crushed

3 tbsp vinegar

6 tbsp sugar

Method

For the cakes

Place all the ingredients for the cake except flour and breadcrumbs in a bowl and mix well. Form walnuts-sized balls and slightly flatten them. Dip in flour-water mixture and then roll in bread crumbs or dry vermicelli. Set aside to dry slightly.

Heat the oil in a thick frying pan and fry cakes in batches, 3-4 at a time. Garnish with crisp fried herbs and serve hot with tomato-chilli jam.

Makes 8 cakes

For tomato-chilli jam

Place all the ingredients in a thick saucepan and cook gently. Reduce to one-third. Use a hand-mixer to blend. Cool. Serve with Thai cakes.

Oriental Vegetables with Peanut Sauce

Ingredients

500 gm vegetables (baby corn, snow peas, broccoli, water chestnuts, capsicums etc.) cut into 2-inch pieces

For the peanut sauce

3 tbsp coarsely-ground peanuts

1 tbsp sesame oil

1 tbsp crushed garlic

1 tbsp crushed ginger

1 tbsp red chilli paste

3-4 kaffir lime leaves, thinly sliced

1 tbsp sesame oil

1 tbsp vinegar

½ cup coconut milk mixed with 1 tsp cornflour

1 tsp raw sugar

1 tsp soy sauce

Salt to taste

To garnish

Sprigs of coriander

Method

For the peanut sauce

Heat oil in a small pan; add garlic, ginger and chilli paste. Fry till fragrant. Add the remaining ingredients and bring to a boil. Remove from heat and set aside.

In a wok, heat oil over high heat and stir-fry the vegetables for 3 to 4 minutes. Add salt. When the vegetables are tender and crisp, pour the peanut sauce over. Toss gently.

Transfer to a serving dish, garnish with coriander sprigs and serve hot.

Serves } 4–6

Oriental Stir-fry Wrap

Ingredients

4 Garlic and Herb Wrappers (recipe follows)

or

6 large lettuce leaves

1 tbsp sesame oil

1 tbsp Thai red curry paste

1 tbsp curry powder

3-4 dried red chillies

200 gm mixed vegetables, cut into strips

200 gm bean curd or cottage cheese cut into small cubes

1 tbsp soy sauce

2-3 tbsp Clear Vegetable Stock (Page 165)

200 gm steamed rice

2-3 tbsp crushed peanuts

Salt, pepper and sugar to taste

1 tbsp lemon juice

2-3 tbsp chopped coriander leaves

3-4 kaffir lime leaves

To serve

Honey-chilli sauce or Red Garlic Sauce (Page 206)

Method

For the filling, heat oil in a wok or heavy frying pan. Add Thai curry paste, curry powder and red chillies and stir-fry for a few seconds. Add the vegetables, bean curd or cottage cheese, soy sauce and the stock. Cook for three to four minutes. The vegetables should remain slightly crunchy. Add the rice, peanuts, salt, pepper, sugar, lemon juice, coriander leaves and lime leaves. Remove from heat and set aside.

Warm each wrap slightly (or lettuce leaf if using) and spread the filling evenly on it. Wrap like a roll and then cut each one diagonally into the required size. Serve immediately with honey-chilli or red garlic sauce.

Serves } 6-8

Garlic and Herb Wrappers

Mix together 1 cup plain flour, ½ tsp each of baking powder and salt, ¼ cup hot water, 1 tbsp butter or margarine and 1 tsp each of garlic powder and mixed herbs. Make a soft dough, divide the dough into 4 parts and roll out each one into a thin round. Cook on a hot griddle, turning to cook both sides. Set aside. To warm the wrappers, pack them tightly in foil and heat in a hot oven for 10 to 15 minutes.

Makes 4 large wrappers

Chinese Barbecue (recipe on page 187)

Vegetable Sui Mai

Ingredients

12-15 wonton wrappers

¾ cup finely-chopped assorted vegetables (carrots, French beans, cauliflower etc.)

6 mushrooms, washed and finely chopped

¼ cup chopped bamboo shoots

1 tbsp sesame oil

1 tbsp crushed ginger

1 tbsp crushed garlic

¼ cup finely-chopped spring onion

A pinch of MSG (optional)

1 tsp rice wine or wine vinegar

1 tbsp cornflour

½ tsp salt

½ tsp sugar

½ tsp pepper

A little cornflour-water paste

To garnish

Finely-chopped coriander leaves

To serve

Soy-chilli sauce

Method

Trim the wonton wrappers to form circles. Cover in a damp piece of muslin to prevent them from drying. Heat the oil in a small frying pan; add ginger, garlic and spring onion and fry for one minute. Add vegetables, mushrooms, bamboo shoots and MSG. Cook until vegetables are soft. Add rice wine, cornflour, salt, sugar and pepper. Remove from heat and set aside to cool.

Spoon the vegetable mixture onto the centre of each wrapper. Bring the ends together and stick them with the help of cornflour paste. Press lightly to ensure that the ends stick together. Set aside to dry for thirty minutes.

Ten to fifteen minutes before serving, bring some water to a boil in a steamer and line the top vessel with coriander leaves. Place the Sui Mai dumplings on them. Steam for seven-eight minutes and serve immediately with soy-chilli sauce.

Serves } 6

Note: Dumplings tend to get dry if not served right away.

Sichuan Fried Rice (recipe on page 197)

Lemon Coriander Soup (recipe on page 162)

Hot and Sour Vegetable Soup (recipe on page 160)

Stuffed Peppers in Black Bean Sauce

Ingredients

4 tbsp oil

1 tbsp ginger-garlic paste

½ cup finely-chopped onion

1 cup finely-chopped and boiled mixed vegetables (carrots, beans, spring onion, cauliflower)

¼ tsp MSG (optional)

2 medium potatoes, boiled and mashed

Salt to taste

Pepper powder to taste

¼ tsp five-spice powder

1 tsp soy sauce

4 medium green capsicums, stemmed, halved and deseeded

1 cup Black Bean Sauce (Page 207)

Method

Heat two tbsp of oil in a frying pan; fry ginger-garlic paste and onion for one minute. Add chopped vegetables and MSG and cook until soft. Add mashed potato, salt, pepper, five-spice powder and soy sauce. Mix well and set aside to cool.

Stuff halved capsicums with this mixture. Heat remaining oil in the same pan, and arrange the capsicums, stuffed side up. Cover and cook over low heat for three minutes. Turn over and cook the other side.

Arrange the capsicums, stuffed side up, in a serving dish and pour the sauce over. Serve hot.

Serves } 4

Eggplant and Tofu in Hot Garlic Sauce

Ingredients

500 gm seedless eggplants (brinjals)

200 gm tofu, cubed

1½ cups Hot Garlic Sauce (Page 207)

4 tbsp oil

2 stalks spring onions, finely chopped

2 dried red chillies

To garnish

2-3 sprigs of coriander and thinly-cut spring onions

Method

Cut the eggplants into two-inch strips directly into a bowl of cold salted water. Heat the oil in a heavy frying pan and fry the eggplant till golden brown. Drain and set aside.

In the remaining oil, fry spring onions and red chillies for a few seconds. Add fried eggplant along with tofu and mix well.

Just before serving, add hot garlic sauce, garnish with coriander and spring onions and serve.

Serves } 4–6

Jade and Ruby in Ginger Sauce

Ingredients

250 gm broccoli florets

2 medium red capsicums cubed

1 tbsp sesame oil

1 tsp crushed garlic

½ tsp red chilli flakes

3 tbsp Clear Vegetable Stock (Page 165)

Salt to taste

To serve

Ginger Sauce (Page 208)

To garnish

Sprigs of coriander and sliced ginger and dried red chillies, fried crisp in oil

Method

Heat oil in a wok; fry garlic with chilli flakes for one minute. Add broccoli, capsicum, stock and salt. Cook until vegetables are tender but crisp.

Just before serving, pour the sauce over the vegetables and garnish with coriander, ginger and chillies.

Serves } 4

Kung Pao Potatoes

Ingredients

300 gm potatoes, peeled and cut into finger chips

For the marinade

1 tbsp soy sauce

2 tsp cornflour

1 tsp oil

¼ tsp salt

¼ tsp pepper powder

For the potatoes

4 tbsp oil

7-8 dried red chillies

½ tsp red chilli flakes

2 inches ginger, minced

3 cloves garlic, minced

⅓ cup Clear Vegetable Stock (Page 165)

1 tbsp cornflour

2 tsp soy sauce

1½ tbsp sugar or plum sauce

Salt to taste

2 tbsp vinegar

2 stalks spring onions cut into 3-inch pieces

Method

Mix potatoes with all the ingredients for the marinade. Cover and set aside for one hour. Heat two tbsp of oil in heavy frying pan and fry potatoes for eight to ten minutes. Drain and set aside.

In the same pan; heat remaining oil, add chillies, chilli flakes, ginger and garlic and fry for three or four minutes. Add the potatoes, vegetable stock mixed with cornflour, soy sauce, sugar or plum sauce, salt and vinegar. Stir to mix. Simmer and add spring onions. Serve hot.

Serves | 4

Note: You can use a mixture of okra and potatoes for a different flavour.

Three Treasure Vegetables

Ingredients

200 gm baby corn cobs

200 gm asparagus

200 gm snow peas

3 tbsp oil

1 tsp finely-chopped garlic

A pinch of MSG (optional)

¾ cup Clear Vegetable Stock (Page 165)

1 tbsp soy sauce

½ tsp salt

½ tsp pepper powder

½ tsp sugar

1 tbsp cornflour mixed with ¼ cup water

Method

Discard the tough ends of the asparagus and use only the tips. Cut all the vegetables diagonally into two-inch pieces.

Heat oil in a wok, fry garlic for a few seconds and add the vegetables with MSG. Stir-fry for two-three minutes.

Add vegetable stock, soy sauce, salt, pepper, sugar and the cornflour mixture. Bring to a boil and serve at once. Do not overcook the vegetables.

Serves 4–6

Note: You can substitute mushrooms for snow peas.

Buddha's Delight

Ingredients

4 tbsp oil

1 tbsp finely-chopped ginger

½ cup sliced bamboo shoots

½ cup sliced straw mushrooms

½ cup sliced bean curd

¼ cup sliced lotus root

½ cup chopped water chestnuts

½ cup washed bean sprouts

½ cup Chinese broccoli, cut into long strips

½ cup Chinese cabbage, cut into long strips

1½ tsp salt

1 tsp sugar

1 tbsp soy sauce

1 tsp rice vinegar

1 tsp cornflour

2 tsp sesame oil

Method

Heat the oil in a heated wok or frying pan. Stir-fry the ginger, bean curd, all the vegetables and salt for three-four minutes. Add sugar, soy sauce and rice vinegar, stirring continuously. If the contents dry out, add a little water.

When the vegetables are cooked, add the cornflour mixed with one tbsp water and bring to a boil. Stir in the sesame oil just before serving.

Serve hot with rice.

Serves | 4–6

Mixed Vegetables in Mustard Sauce

Ingredients

2 medium carrots cut into cubes

½ cup French beans cut into ½-inch pieces

6-8 baby corn cobs cut into ½-inch pieces

1 medium capsicum cut into cubes

¼ cup water chestnuts cut into pieces

2 tbsp sesame oil

A pinch of MSG (optional)

1 cup Mustard Sauce (Page 208)

Salt to taste

To garnish

A few sprigs of coriander leaves

Method

Heat oil in a wok and stir-fry the vegetables with MSG. Cook over high heat for three-four minutes. Add mustard sauce and salt if required. Garnish and serve at once.

Serves | 4

Fluffy Fried Vegetables in Hot and Sweet Sauce

Ingredients

1 cup mixed finely chopped vegetables (cabbage, French beans, carrots and onions)

2 tbsp cornflour

2 tbsp plain flour

A pinch of MSG (optional)

Salt and pepper to taste

Oil for frying

1½ cups Hot and Sweet Sauce (Page 206)

Method

Mix the vegetables and both kinds of flour along with MSG, salt and pepper. Shape the mixture into flat dumplings and fry in hot oil until crisp.

When ready to serve, place the dumplings in a serving dish and pour hot and sweet sauce over and serve at once.

Serves | 4

Sautéed Chinese Greens

Ingredients

500 gm Chinese cabbage (pak choy)

1-2 slices ginger, finely chopped

3 tbsp oil

1 tsp salt

1 tsp sugar

1 tbsp soy sauce

2 tbsp finely-chopped garlic

½ cup finely-chopped spring onions

Method

Wash the pak choy and cut off the tough ends. Cut the leaves into quarter-inch lengths.

Heat a wok and add oil. When hot, add chopped pak choy, spring onions, ginger and garlic. Fry for one minute. Add salt, sugar and soy sauce. Cook for two more minutes.

Serve at once.

Serves | 4–6

Vegetable Balls in Manchurian Sauce

Ingredients

For the vegetable balls

2 cups finely-chopped cabbage

2 medium carrots, grated

3-4 stalks spring onions, finely chopped

1 medium onion, finely chopped

3 cloves garlic, finely chopped

1 green chilli, finely chopped

2 tbsp cornflour

4 tbsp plain flour

Salt to taste

¼ tsp pepper

A pinch of MSG (optional)

Oil for deep frying

2 cups Manchurian Sauce (Page 208)

Method

For the vegetable balls, mix cabbage, carrots, onion, spring onions, garlic, green chilli, both types of flour, salt, pepper and MSG. Shape mixture into small balls. Heat oil in a frying pan and fry the balls in hot oil until golden brown. Drain and set aside.

To serve
Heat the Manchurian sauce, add fried balls and simmer for a few minutes and serve hot with rice or noodles.

Serves 4–6

Asparagus, Broccoli and Water Chestnuts in Coriander Sauce

Ingredients

200 gm fresh asparagus spears

200 gm fresh broccoli florets

200 gm fresh water chestnuts

1 cup coriander sauce

1 tbsp oil

2-3 cloves garlic, chopped

3-4 stalks spring onions, cut into 1-inch pieces

Method

Cut the asparagus in one-inch lengths. Discard the tough ends and use only the tips. Cut the broccoli into bite-sized pieces. Remove skin from water chestnuts and cut into half.

Heat the oil in a wok and add garlic and spring onions. Fry till the leaves wilt. Add all the vegetables and MSG. Cook till vegetables are tender but firm.

Just before serving, add the coriander sauce to the vegetables and bring to a boil. Serve immediately.

Serves 6

Chinese Barbecue

Ingredients

4 cups mixed vegetables. Choose from the following:

Bean sprouts, washed and drained

Cabbage, shredded

Carrots, shredded

Red, green or yellow capsicums cut into thin strips

Spring onions, chopped

Onions, sliced then halved

Baby corn cobs, cut vertically

Asparagus spears, cut into 3-inch pieces

Yellow corn kernels, boiled

Mushrooms, washed and sliced

Snow peas, washed and halved

Bean curd, cut into long strips

For the seasoning

1 tbsp vinegar

1 tsp chopped green chillies

2 tbsp sesame or peanut oil

1 tbsp chilli powder

1 tbsp finely-chopped ginger

2 tbsp finely-chopped garlic

1 tbsp sesame seeds, toasted

1 tbsp powdered peanuts

1 tbsp powdered sugar

2 tbsp soy sauce

¼ cup water

Salt to taste

1 cups steamed rice or boiled noodles

To serve

Chilli-garlic Sauce (Page 207)

Method

Place the vegetables in a large bowl. Mix together the vinegar and green chilies in a small bowl. In a separate bowl mix the sesame or peanut oil and chilli powder.

Add the seasoning ingredients and stir-fry the mixture in a wok over high heat for four or five minutes if you like the vegetables to be crunchy, and seven or eight minutes if you like them to be well-cooked. Add rice or noodles.

Serve immediately with chilli-garlic sauce.

Serves } 2

Spicy Lady's Fingers

Ingredients

300 gm lady's fingers slit vertically

½ cup boiled corn kernels

2 cups thick coconut milk

4 tbsp oil

Spice paste

10 red chillies (fresh or dried)

2 stalks lemon grass

1 inch galangal

4 cloves garlic

8-10 shallots

Salt to taste

To garnish

2-3 stems spring onions

Method

Sprinkle two tbsp of oil on ladies' fingers and steam them.

Grind all the ingredients for the spice paste. Fry the spice paste in remaining oil and add two tbsp of coconut milk. Cook until fragrant.

Add ladies' fingers and cook till soft. Add remaining coconut milk, corn and salt.

Garnish with spring onions and serve hot.

Serves } 4

Korean Kimchi

Ingredients

500 gm cabbage, cut into cubes

250 gm cucumber, cut into 2-inch sticks

2 tbsp salt

4 cups cold water

2 cups hot water

For the pickling mixture

1½ tbsp minced spring onion

1 tbsp minced ginger

1 tbsp minced garlic

1½ tbsp ground fresh red chillies or chilli flakes

2 tsp sugar

2 tsp vinegar

2 tsp sesame oil

1 tsp salt

Method

Separate the cabbage layers, sprinkle salt and soak in cold water. Cover and set aside for three to four hours. Rinse well and squeeze out excess liquid.

Boil two cups of water and pour over the pickling mixture. Mix this with the cabbage and cucumber. Fill in a glass jar and refrigerate overnight.

Serve with any Oriental meal.

Makes 4 cups

Hormok Fak

(Vegetables with Spicy Coconut Sauce)

Ingredients

For the vegetables

100 gm French beans, chopped and blanched

100 gm broccoli, chopped and blanched

1 cup bean sprouts, washed and blanched

½ cup shallots, sliced

1 tbsp oil

For the spicy coconut sauce

7 bird's eye chillies, sliced

8 fresh red chillies, sliced

1 tbsp chopped galangal

1 tbsp chopped lemon grass

4 cloves garlic

4 shallots, peeled and sliced

1 inch fresh turmeric, peeled and sliced

1 tbsp sugar

3-4 kaffir lime leaves

3 cups tender coconut flesh

3 cups tender coconut water

1 tsp cornflour

Salt to taste

Method

For the sauce

Grind together both the chillies, galangal, lemon grass, garlic, shallots, turmeric, lime leaves and sugar.

Blend coconut flesh with water and make a smooth thick cream.

Mix one tsp cornflour with coconut cream and the ground paste. Place the mixture in a pan and simmer until thick.

For the vegetables

Heat oil in a wok and fry the shallots until browned. Add beans and broccoli. Cook till coated with oil. Pour the sauce over the vegetables and fill the mixture into a cleaned coconut shell.

Serve hot with rice.

Serves 6

Tip: Reserve the tender coconut shell after removing the coconut flesh and water. Wash the shell well and use to serve.

Vegetable Rendang

Dry Malaysian Curry

Ingredients

For the curry

3 cups chopped mixed vegetables, boiled

8 tbsp oil

2 tbsp curry powder mixed with a little water

½ cup thick coconut milk

1 tbsp soy sauce

1 tbsp sugar

¼ cup grated fresh coconut, fried in a little oil

For the spice paste

20 dried red chillies

2 tbsp galangal, chopped

1 stalk lemon grass, finely chopped

3-4 cloves garlic

4-5 kaffir lime leaves

½ cup shallots

5-6 almonds

1 tbsp salt

Method

Put all the ingredients for the spice paste in a spice grinder and make a paste with a little water. Heat oil in a saucepan; fry the paste and curry powder till fragrant. Add half the coconut milk and cook till the oil separates.

Add the vegetables, soy sauce, salt and sugar. Mix well. Add the fried coconut and the remaining coconut milk.

Cook for eight to ten minutes and serve hot with rice or bread.

Serves } 6

Massaman Curry

Ingredients

For the curry

2 medium potatoes, parboiled, peeled and cubed

½ cup chopped pumpkin, boiled

5-6 small onions, halved

1 cup yellow corn, boiled

2 tbsp tamarind juice

1 tsp salt

1 tbsp sugar

1 cup coconut milk

½ cup coconut cream

1 tbsp cornflour

300 gm whole fresh peanuts, shelled and boiled

2 tbsp oil

2-3 tbsp Massaman Curry Paste (recipe below)

For the curry paste

10 dried red chillies, deseeded and chopped

1 tsp coriander seed powder

1 tsp cumin seed powder

1 tsp cinnamon powder

1 tsp clove powder

1 tsp star anise powder

1 tsp cardamom powder

1 tsp white pepper powder

4 tbsp chopped shallots

4 tbsp chopped garlic

2-inch stalk lemon grass, chopped

½ inch galangal, chopped

1 tbsp chopped kaffir lime leaves

1 tsp salt

¼ cup water

Method

For the curry paste

In a dry frying pan, roast all the powdered spices and chillies over low heat until fragrant.

Transfer to a mortar with the rest of the ingredients and pound to a fine paste.

Transfer to a bowl and set aside.

Makes ¾ cup

For the curry

Heat the oil in a pan and fry the paste for a few minutes. Add all the vegetables, coconut milk, peanuts, salt, sugar, tamarind juice and cornflour mixed with three tbsp of water. Bring to a boil. Add coconut cream and simmer for three or four minutes. Do not over boil or the coconut milk will curdle.

Serve hot with rice.

Serves 4-6

Balinese Vegetable Curry

Ingredients

For the paste

12 pieces shallots

2 tbsp (each) finely-chopped galangal or ginger and garlic

1 tbsp turmeric powder or 2″ piece fresh turmeric root

½ cup Macadamia nuts or candle nuts

1 stalk kemon grass, finely chopped

1 tbsp (each) coriander powder and tomato paste

3 pieces (each) large red chillies and bird's eye chillies

2 tbsp tamarind pulp

½ cup water

For the curry

3-4 tbsp sesame or grape seed oil

3-4 pieces kaffir lime leaves, chopped

1 cup (each) Vegetable Stock (Page...) and thick coconut milk

1 cup cauliflower florets, blanched in salted water

1 cup yellow and green pumpkin, cut into cubes and boiled

3-4 small brinjals, cut and sautéed

½ cup boiled green peas

Salt and pepper to taste

To Garnish

Fried shallots

Method

For the paste

In a food processor or wet grinder, purée all the ingredients with water until smooth and set aside.

For the curry

Prepare the vegetables as per instructions.

Heat oil in a heavy saucepan; fry the paste until fragrant, about 5 minutes. Add kaffir lime leaves, stock and coconut milk. Bring to a gentle boil. Add prepared vegetables, salt and pepper. Bring to a boil and remove from stove.

Garnish with fried shallots. Serve hot with steamed or fried rice.

Serves 6

Note: To make fried shallots, toss 1 cup sliced shallots with ½ cup rice flour. Fry in hot oil until crisp. Remove and drain on paper towel. Season with salt.

Roti Canai with Malay Curry

Ingredients

500 gm plain flour, sifted

½ tsp sugar

½ tsp salt

½ cup water

1 egg or ¼ cup milk

½ cup butter

To serve
Malay Curry (recipe follows)

Method

Mix together flour, sugar and salt. Make a soft dough with water and egg or milk. Shape into six small balls; cover the dough with half the butter and leave to stand overnight.

When you want to make the rotis, work with one portion at a time; knead and roll out as thin as possible. Cook on an inverted round-bottomed vessel or iron griddle till brown specks appear. Brush a little butter on each one while cooking. Turn over and cook the other side as well.

Serve hot with Malay curry.

Makes 6 rotis

Malay Curry

Ingredients

2 tbsp oil
6-8 shallots, chopped
2 tbsp red chilli-garlic paste
2 tbsp curry powder
2 stalks spring onions cut into 2-inch pieces
½ cup blanched broccoli florets
½ cup cubed potatoes
2 tbsp brown sugar
3 cups thin coconut milk
2-3 tbsp tamarind pulp
Salt to taste

Method

Heat the oil in a saucepan and fry the shallots and chilli-garlic paste. Add curry powder and fry for two to three minutes. Add spring onions, broccoli and the potatoes. Mix well and cook for a minute. Add brown sugar, coconut milk, tamarind pulp and salt. Bring to a boil. Serve hot with roti or rice.

Makes 3-4 cups

Eight Jewel Fried Rice

Ingredients

2 cups rice, washed and soaked for ½ an hour

6 cups water

4 tbsp sesame oil

1 tbsp finely-chopped ginger

1 tbsp finely-chopped garlic

1 tbsp finely-chopped green chillies

¼ cup chopped mushrooms

¼ cup chopped carrots

¼ cup chopped French beans

¼ cup chopped spring onions

¼ cup chopped cauliflower

¼ cup chopped capsicum

Salt to taste

A pinch of MSG (optional)

⅓ cup shelled and boiled green peas and corn kernels

1 tbsp soy sauce

2 tbsp sliced and fried almonds

Method

Bring the water to a rolling boil and gently pour the rice into it in a thin stream. Cook briskly till just tender. Drain and set aside.

Heat the oil in a wok and fry ginger, garlic and green chillies for one minute. Add mushrooms, carrots, beans, spring onions, cauliflower and capsicum along with salt and MSG (if using). Cook until soft.

Add rice, peas, corn and soy sauce. Stir gently to mix.

Turn out on to a serving plate and garnish with almonds. Serve hot.

Serves } 6

Sichuan Fried Rice

Ingredients

2 cups rice, washed and soaked in water

5 tbsp oil

¼ cup finely-chopped carrot

¼ cup finely-chopped cabbage

¼ cup finely-chopped mushroom

¼ cup finely-chopped water chestnuts

¼ cup finely-chopped green capsicum

¼ cup finely-chopped bean sprouts

2-3 stalks spring onions, finely chopped

A pinch of MSG (optional)

1 tbsp finely-chopped ginger

1 tbsp finely-chopped garlic

1 tsp vinegar

2 whole dried red chillies

1 tsp chilli paste

2 tbsp tomato purée

1 tbsp soy sauce

Salt and pepper to taste

To garnish

3-4 tbsp fried mixed nuts

Method

Cook rice in plenty of water and salt till tender. Drain, add cold water and drain again.

Heat oil in a wok; add all the vegetables, MSG (if using), ginger, garlic, vinegar, whole dried red chillies, chilli paste, tomato purée, soy sauce, salt and pepper. Cook until vegetables are tender. Add cooked rice and mix gently. Garnish with nuts and serve hot.

Serves } 4–6

Burnt Garlic Fried Rice

Ingredients

4 cups steamed rice

3 large cloves garlic, chopped

3-4 tbsp oil

1 tsp garlic paste

1 tbsp soy sauce

To garnish
Sliced spring onions

Method

Heat oil in a frying pan; fry garlic until golden brown. Remove and set aside.

In the same pan, fry garlic paste, add steamed rice and soy sauce. Mix gently. Cook till the rice is heated through and well-coated with oil.

Transfer to a serving plate and sprinkle burnt garlic all over the rice. Garnish with spring onions and serve immediately.

Serves } 4

Nasi Goreng

Malaysian Fried Rice

Ingredients

1 cup rice, washed, soaked and cooked in 2 cups water

¼ cup oil

2 medium onions, chopped

2-3 cloves garlic

3-4 red chilles, deseeded (fresh or dried)

1 inch ginger, chopped

4 tbsp boiled green peas

2 tbsp grated fresh coconut

2 tbsp soy sauce

2 tbsp lemon juice

1 tsp sugar

Salt to taste

Pepper to taste

To garnish

Coarsely chopped salted peanuts, sliced tomatoes and onions

Method

Purée onions, garlic, chillies and ginger in a blender. Heat the oil in a wok and fry the paste. Cook for five to seven minutes, stirring occasionally.

Add the peas, rice, coconut, soy sauce, lemon juice, sugar, salt and pepper. Cook until the mixture is heated through and rice is coated well with the spice.

Transfer rice to a serving dish and garnish with peanuts, tomatoes and onions.

Serves } 4

Khao Ngop

Grilled Curried Rice

Ingredients

2 cups steamed rice

1 tbsp red curry paste

1 tbsp oil

$^2/_3$ cup chopped mushrooms

2-3 small aubergines (eggplants/ brinjals), chopped

4-5 baby corn cobs, chopped

8-10 French beans cut into ½-inch pieces

½ cup coconut cream mixed with 1 tsp cornflour

½ tsp salt

2 kaffir lime leaves, finely chopped

10 basil leaves

2 pieces banana leaves

Method

Heat oil in a pan; stir-fry the vegetables until tender, but crisp.

Place coconut cream in a large bowl and stir in the red curry paste until thoroughly blended. Add the cooked vegetables, stir well and add salt, kaffir lime leaves and basil. Add the rice and mix.

Place the rice on a banana leaf and fold it like a packet and grill in the oven for seven to eight minutes. Remove from oven and serve immediately on a fresh banana leaf.

Serves } 4

Chop Suey

Ingredients

2 cups crispy noodles

or

1 cup boiled noodles and 1 cup fried noodles

4 tbsp oil

1 carrot, shredded

1 capsicum, shredded

12-15 French beans, cut into 2-inch thin, long pieces

¾ cup shredded cabbage

3-4 stalks spring onions, finely chopped

¼ tsp MSG (optional)

2 cups bean sprouts, washed

Salt and pepper to taste

For the sauce

4 large tomatoes, chopped

2 cloves garlic

1 medium onion

½ tsp five-spice powder

3 tbsp powdered sugar

¼ cup vinegar

1 cup water

1 tbsp soy sauce

2 tbsp corn flour

1 tsp chilli sauce

To garnish

A few tomato wedges

Method

For the sauce, pressure-cook the tomatoes along with garlic, onion, and five-spice powder. Cool and strain. Add the rest of the ingredients and bring to a boil stirring continuously. Simmer for two or three minutes. Remove from heat and set aside to cool.

Heat the oil in a wok; add carrot, capsicum, French beans, cabbage, spring onions and MSG. Cook for two-three minutes. Add bean sprouts, salt and pepper. Cook for another three or four minutes. Add the sauce, boiled noodles and half the fried noodles and mix well.

Transfer to a serving plate and sprinkle remaining fried noodles on top. Garnish with tomato wedges. Serve immediately.

Serves } 4

Hot and Spicy Hawkers' Noodles

Ingredients

200 gm narrow flat noodles or Hakka noodles

2 cups crispy noodles

2 tsp sesame oil

1 tbsp finely-chopped garlic

1 tbsp finely-chopped red chilles

1 tbsp finely-chopped ginger

2 stalks spring onions, finely chopped

1 cup bean sprouts

1 cup shredded carrots

1 cup onions

1 cup Clear Vegetable Stock (Page 165)

2-3 tbsp finely-sliced coconut

2 tbsp soy sauce

2 tbsp rice vinegar

1 tsp salt

1 tsp pepper powder

1 tsp chilli oil

2-3 tbsp finely chopped coriander

To Serve

Sichuan Sauce (Page 206)

Method

Heat the oil in a frying pan and stir-fry garlic, red chillies, ginger and spring onions for one minute. Add bean sprouts, carrots, onions, stock and sliced coconut and cook until soft. Add soy sauce, vinegar, salt, pepper and chilli oil.

Just before serving, blanch the flat or Hakka noodles in boiling water, drain and place in a serving bowl. Pour the vegetable mixture over the noodles. Sprinkle crispy noodles and coriander on top and serve hot with Sichuan sauce on the side.

Serves } 4

To make crispy noodles, boil Hakka noodles following the instructions on the package, drain and fry in hot oil. Store in an airtight container.

Mee Goreng

Malaysian Chilli Noodles

Ingredients

200 gm thin wheat noodles

4 tbsp oil

2-3 fresh red chillies, slit

2-3 green chillies, slit

2 medium tomatoes cut into wedges

4 stalks spring onions cut lengthways

1 cup shredded Chinese cabbage

1 cup bean sprouts, washed

2 tbsp light soy sauce

Salt to taste

Spice paste

6-8 dried red chillies

1 cup grated onion

4 cloves garlic

1 tsp salt

1 tbsp sugar

2 tbsp chopped galangal

1 tbsp tomato sauce

To garnish

Fried shallots and lemon wedges

Method

Bring a large pan of water to a boil and cook the noodles for three minutes. Drain and set aside.

Grind all the ingredients for the spice paste. Heat oil in a wok and fry the spice paste, chillies, tomatoes and spring onions till slightly wilted. Add the cabbage and the bean sprouts. Cook for one minute. Sprinkle a little water if you find the mixture too dry.

Add the noodles, soy sauce and salt. Mix well.

Transfer the noodles to a serving dish and garnish with fried shallots and lemon wedges. Serve hot.

Serves } 4

Spicy Stir-fried Noodles with Curry Sauce

Ingredients

For the noodles

200 gm broad noodles, boiled

1 cup bean sprouts, washed and drained

4-5 mushrooms, sliced

½ cup French beans cut into 1-inch pieces

2 stalks spring onions cut into 1-inch pieces

3-4 fresh red chillies

10 cloves garlic

2 tbsp oil

2 dried red chillies

1 tbsp soy sauce

1 tsp salt

1 tsp sugar

A few basil leaves

For the curry sauce

1 cup coconut milk

1 tbsp red curry paste

1 tsp curry powder

1 stalk spring onion, finely-chopped

1 tbsp roasted and crushed peanuts

1 tbsp tamarind juice

1-2 stalks lemon grass

½ tsp sugar

To garnish

Crispy potato sticks

Method

For the noodles

Make a paste of fresh red chillies, garlic and a little salt. Set aside.

In a wok, heat the oil. Fry chilli-garlic paste for a few seconds. Add dried chillies along with all the vegetables. Cook until vegetables are tender but crisp. Add boiled noodles, salt, sugar, soy sauce and basil leaves. Continue cooking till the noodles are heated through and the ingredients are mixed well.

Garnish with crispy potato sticks and serve hot with curry sauce.

For the curry sauce

In a pan, gently heat the coconut milk, stir in the red curry paste until thoroughly blended. Add the remaining ingredients, stirring until mixed. Serve hot with the noodles.

Serves } 4

Table Sauces

WHOLE GARLIC SAUCE
Heat 2 tbsp oil in a saucepan and stir-fry 20 garlic cloves and 1 tbsp red chilli paste for two minutes. Lower heat and add 2 tbsp tomato purée, ¾ cup water, ½ tsp pepper, salt to taste and 1 tsp soy sauce. Simmer for two-three minutes. Add 1 tbsp cornflour mixed with ¼ cup water, stirring all the time, until the sauce thickens. Cool and pour into a bowl.

Makes 1 cup

SOY-CHILLI SAUCE
Heat 2 tbsp oil in a pan until it smokes; add 1 tbsp finely-chopped green chillies, 1 tsp finely-chopped ginger, 1 tsp finely-chopped garlic and 1 tbsp finely-chopped spring onion. Add ¼ cup soy sauce, 2 tbsp water, ½ tsp vinegar and 1 tsp sugar and stir. Set aside to cool. Transfer to a serving bowl.

Makes ½ cup

GINGER-CHILLI SAUCE
Heat 2 tbsp oil in a small pan and fry 4 tbsp finely-grated ginger, 2 tbsp finely-chopped green chillies, 4 cloves crushed garlic, 1 tbsp finely-chopped coriander leaves and 2 tbsp finely-chopped spring onion for two minutes. Add ½ tsp sugar, ½ tsp salt, ½ tsp white pepper powder, 1 tsp vinegar and ¼ cup water and bring to a boil. Remove from heat and set aside to cool. Transfer to a serving bowl.

Makes ½ cup

GREEN CHILLI-GARLIC SAUCE
In a bowl, mix together 6-7 finely-chopped green chillies, 6-8 cloves finely-chopped garlic, 2 tbsp finely-chopped coriander leaves, 1 tbsp powdered sugar, 2 tsp white vinegar, ½ cup water, juice of 1 lemon and salt to taste. Leave to stand for fifteen minutes before serving.

Makes ¾ cup

CHILLIES IN VINEGAR
Pour ½ cup brown or white vinegar into a serving bowl. Add ¼ cup finely-sliced green chillies and ½ tsp each of salt and sugar. Stir well. Leave to stand for three-four hours before using.

Makes ¾ cup

Note: You can also add two tbsp finely-chopped ginger along with the chillies.

SPICY CHILLI OIL

Combine 6 dried red chillies, 2 tbsp chilli powder, 1 tsp coarsely-powdered peppercorns, 1 tbsp each finely-chopped ginger and garlic and 2 tbsp finely-chopped spring onion, in a bowl and set aside. Heat ¾ cup sesame oil in a small saucepan till it begins to smoke. Remove from heat and add all the ingredients. Mix well. Cover and set aside for four hours. Strain and pour into a bottle. Serve as an accompaniment to soup or as a topping on vegetable or noodle dishes.

Makes ¾ cup

RED GARLIC SAUCE

Heat 2 tbsp oil in a small saucepan. Fry 1 tbsp finely-chopped garlic, 2 tbsp finely-chopped spring onions, 1 tsp finely-chopped green chillies and 1 tbsp finely-chopped onions and sauté for three to five minutes till soft. Add 1 tbsp red chilli paste, 2 tbsp tomato purée, 1 tsp soy sauce, a pinch of MSG (optional), 1 tsp sugar, ½ tsp vinegar and salt to taste. Cook for two to three minutes and let it cool to room temperature.

Makes 1 cup

HOT AND SWEET SAUCE

Heat 2 tbsp oil in a pan; fry 2 tbsp ginger, garlic and green-chilli paste. Add 2 tbsp grated onion and fry for two minutes. Add ½ cup tomato purée, ²/₃ cup water, ½ tsp pepper, 1 tsp chilli powder, salt to taste and 2 tbsp sugar. Stir well. Bring to a boil and add 1 tbsp cornflour mixed with three to four tbsp of water and cook until thick. Remove from heat and leave to cool.

Makes 1½ cups

SAMBAL

Mix 24 soaked dried red chillies, 2 tbsp crushed garlic, 4 tbsp lemon juice, 1 tbsp powdered sugar, 1 tsp salt and 2 tbsp oil in a mortar and pestle and crush to make a thick paste. Transfer to a serving bowl and add ¼ cup water. Serve with soups, noodles or rice dishes.

Makes ²/₃ cup

SICHUAN SAUCE

Grind together 20 soaked red chillies with 5 cloves of garlic to a smooth paste. Heat 3 tbsp of oil in a frying pan. Add 1 tbsp chopped garlic, 1 tsp chopped green chilli, 1 tsp grated ginger, 2 tbsp chopped onions and fry for 1 minute. Add the paste and fry again. Add 1 tbsp vinegar with ½ cup vegetable stock. Mix well. Add 2 tsp sugar, 2 tsp lemon juice, salt, MSG (optional), and 1 tbsp corn flour mixed with 2 tbsp of water. Cook for 1 minute stirring constantly. Serve hot.

Makes 1 ½ cups

Cooking Sauces

SWEET AND SOUR SAUCE

Mix ½ cup tomato sauce, ¼ cup vinegar, 2½ tbsp brown sugar, 1 cup water, 1 tsp soy sauce, 2 tbsp cornflour, ½ tsp pepper and salt to taste in a saucepan and stir well. Cook over low heat, stirring constantly. When it begins to boil, simmer for two minutes. Stir in 1 tsp sesame oil. Remove and cool. Serve with soups and starters or with vegetables.

Makes 1½ cups

CHILLI-GARLIC SAUCE

Process 12-15 soaked dried red chillies, 6 cloves chopped garlic, 6 tbsp white vinegar, 2 tsp sugar and 1 tsp salt in a blender until fine. Add 1 tbsp sesame oil and store refrigerated in a covered jar. Serve as a dipping sauce with snacks or other cooked dishes.

Makes 1 cup

BLACK BEAN SAUCE

Crush 1 tbsp soaked and boiled black beans lightly and mix with ¾ cup boiling water mixed with ½ vegetable stock cube, 2 tsp cornflour, 1 tsp sugar, ½ tsp grated ginger, 2 tbsp vinegar, 1 tbsp soy sauce, 1 clove crushed garlic, salt and pepper to taste and 1 tsp melted butter. Stir until all the ingredients are well-blended. Bring to a boil and simmer until thick.

Makes 1 cup

HOT GARLIC SAUCE

Make a smooth paste of 2-3 dried red chillies broken into pieces and 1 tbsp garlic paste with a little water. Mix 1 tbsp cornflour and one cup of water. Heat 2 tbsp oil in a pan and fry the chilli-garlic paste for one minute. Add 1 tbsp vinegar, ¼ cup tomato purée, 1 tbsp soy sauce, ½ tsp salt, ½ tsp pepper, a pinch of sugar and a pinch of MSG (optional). Cook for one minute. Add the cornflour mixture and stir continuously until thick. Use as required.

Makes 1½ cups

GINGER SAUCE

Mix together 1½ tbsp cornflour with ¼ cup water. In a pan, heat 1 tbsp oil and add 1 tbsp finely-chopped ginger and 1 tsp green chilli paste. Fry for one minute. Add ½ cup tomato purée, ½ cup Clear Vegetable Stock (Page 165), 1 tsp soy sauce and 1 tsp chilli sauce. Bring to a boil and add cornflour mixture, 1 tsp vinegar, 1 tsp sugar and salt and pepper to taste. Cook till the sauce thickens.

Makes 1 cup

MUSTARD SAUCE

Mix 1 tbsp mustard powder, 1 cup Clear Vegetable Stock (Page 165), ½ tsp salt, ½ tsp sugar, 1 tbsp cornflour and a pinch of dried thyme in a small pan and bring to a boil, stirring continuously. Cook until thick.

Makes 1 cup

MANCHURIAN SAUCE

Heat 2 tbsp oil in a small saucepan; fry 1 finely-chopped medium onion, 1 tbsp finely-chopped garlic, 1 tbsp finely-chopped ginger, 1 tbsp finely-chopped green chillies, 1 tbsp finely-chopped dried red chilli and a pinch of MSG (optional) for two-three minutes. Add 1 cup Clear Vegetable Stock (Page 165), 2 tsp soy sauce, ½ tsp sugar, ½ tsp salt and ½ tsp pepper and bring to a boil. Add ½ tsp chilli sauce and 2 tbsp cornflour mixed with ¼ cup water and boil until thick. Sprinkle 2 stalks finely-chopped spring onions and stir well. Remove from heat and set aside to cool.

Makes 1 ½ cups

Note: You can also make vegetable stock with one cup water and one vegetable stock cube.

Continental

Continental cuisine is generally the cuisine of Western Europe, including France and Spain. There are regional variations within each country as well! Not only is this region renowned for superb wines, but also for its breads, cheeses, appetisers, soups and salads; its quiches and pies and a huge variety of desserts. Feast on Cream of Split Peas, Mushroom and Broccoli Vol-au-Vent, Corn and Potato Rösti and Chocolate Truffles...

Spring Vegetable Soup

Ingredients

2 pieces (each) onions, potatoes and leeks, cut into cubes

2 tbsp butter

1 stem spring onion, finely chopped

100 gm (each) cauliflower, asparagus and carrots, chopped

¼ cup green peas, coarsely chopped

5-6 French beans, chopped

1 tbsp wholewheat flour

1 cup Vegetable Stock (Page 245)

1 cup milk

2 tbsp grated Cheddar cheese

Salt and pepper to taste

To serve

Crusty garlic and herb wholewheat bread

Method

Cook onions, potatoes and leeks along with 6 cups of water in a pressure cooker for three whistles. When cooked liquidize, strain and set aside.

In a saucepan melt butter and fry spring onions, cauliflower, asparagus, carrots, green peas and French beans. Cook until soft. Add wholewheat flour, followed by the onion-potato liquidized soup and vegetable stock. Boil until the vegetables are cooked. Add milk, cheese, salt and pepper. Serve hot with garlic and herb bread.

Serves } 6-8

Tomato Vichyssoise

Ingredients

2 tbsp butter

6½ cups Vegetable Stock (Page 245) or water

1 large leek, white part only, thinly sliced

1 bay leaf

½ tsp dried thyme

500 gm baby potatoes, peeled and halved

Salt to taste

4 tbsp olive oil

500 gm tomatoes, blanched and chopped

1 cup whole basil leaves

Salt, pepper and wine vinegar to taste

Method

Melt butter in a saucepan with ½ cup of stock or water. Add leek, bay leaf and thyme and cook for 4-5 minutes. Add the potatoes, salt and remaining stock or water; cover and cook till potatoes are soft. Remove from heat and pass the soup through a sieve. (Do not liquidize).

In a separate pan, heat 1 tbsp of oil and cook the tomatoes with a little salt until slightly soft. Remove, cool and pass through a sieve and add to the soup. Return the soup to the stove and bring to a boil. Add salt, pepper and wine vinegar to taste.

Make a paste with basil and the remaining olive oil in a blender and set aside. Ladle the soup into bowls and swirl a spoonful of the basil mixture in each bowl. Serve hot.

Serves } 6

Note: You may also add milk, cream or stock to thin the soup further.

Crème de Petits Pois

Cream of Split Peas

Ingredients

2 tbsp butter

100 gm onions, finely chopped

2 cloves garlic, minced

200 gm split green peas, soaked in water for 6 hours

100 gm shelled green peas (frozen or fresh)

2 cups Vegetable Stock (Page 245)

Salt and pepper to taste

1 tbsp spinach purée

½ cup milk + cream

For chives cream

3 tbsp (each) freshly chopped chives and thick yogurt

½ tsp (each) salt and sugar

To garnish

A few chives and finely-chopped red capsicum

To serve

Multigrain toasted bread

Method

Melt butter in a saucepan and sauté onion and garlic until translucent. Add soaked split peas, fresh or frozen peas and vegetable stock. Bring to a boil and simmer until peas are cooked. Alternatively, place the whole mixture in a pressure cooker and cook for 3 whistles. Cool the mixture, liquidize and sieve.

Return the soup to the saucepan and add salt, pepper, spinach purée and boil once again. Add milk and cream and heat gently.

To make chives cream blend chives and yogurt in a small blender jar. Add salt and sugar and refrigerate until ready to use.

To serve, ladle the soup into individual soup bowls, swirl the chive cream around, sprinkle red capsicum in the middle and place the long stem of the chive across the bowl. Serve with multigrain bread.

Serves } 4–6

Roasted Cauliflower Soup

Ingredients

1 kg cauliflower, cut into florets

2 medium onions cut into cubes

3-4 cloves garlic

2 tbsp olive oil

½ tsp (each) salt and pepper

2½ tsp fresh thyme

2 cups Vegetable Stock (Page 245)

1½ cups milk + cream

Salt to taste

To garnish
Sprig of thyme and fresh cream

To serve
Crusty bread (baguette)

Method

Preheat the oven to 425°F/220°C/Gas Mark 7.

Toss cauliflower, onions and garlic together in a large roasting pan. Drizzle the vegetables with oil; season them with salt, pepper and thyme. Toss lightly to coat. Roast in the oven for 20 minutes or under the grill for 7-8 minutes, stirring occasionally, until they turn golden brown.

Remove from oven and place them in a large saucepan with vegetable stock and bring to a boil and then simmer for 5 minutes. Add the milk, cream and salt. Purée the soup in a blender, transfer to a saucepan and heat through. Pour in individual bowls and garnish with sprig of thyme and cream. Serve with crusty baguette.

Serves 8

Tomato Orange Soup

Ingredients

50 gm butter

2 medium onions, finely chopped

1 kg tomatoes, quartered

4 tbsp orange juice

1 small bay leaf

1 tsp brown sugar

Salt and pepper to taste

2 tsp finely-chopped basil leaves

1 tbsp sherry (optional)

To garnish
A bunch of basil leaves

Note: If the soup is too thick after liquidizing add ½ cup water or stock before boiling.

Method

Melt butter in a saucepan over gentle heat, add the onion and cook until transparent but not browned. Add the tomatoes, orange juice and bay leaf. Bring to a boil and then simmer for 15 minutes, or until tomatoes have turned into a pulp. Rub through a sieve and return the purée to a clean pan. Bring to a boil; add sugar, salt, pepper and basil. Add sherry, if using.

Garnish with basil leaves and serve hot with wholewheat toast.

Serves } 4

French Onion Soup

Ingredients

4 large onions, finely chopped

¼ cup butter

1½ tbsp cornflour

4 cups Brown Vegetable Stock (recipe follows)

Salt and pepper to taste

A few drops of Worcestershire sauce

1 tbsp sherry (optional)

6 slices crusty bread

6 tbsp grated cheese

Method

Heat the butter in a heavy saucepan; sauté onions until golden brown. Remove from pan and set aside. In the same pan add cornflour and cook for 1-2 minutes. Remove from heat and gradually add the stock. Return to stove and bring the soup to a boil. Add salt, pepper, Worcestershire sauce and sherry if using. Set aside until ready.

To serve, sprinkle cheese on the bread and place the slices under the grill until cheese has melted. Alternatively, spoon the soup into 6 ovenproof soup bowls. Place a bread slice on top of each one and place the bowls under a very hot grill until the cheese melts. Serve immediately.

Brown Vegetable Stock

Ingredients

2 tbsp oil

4 pieces (each) carrots and celery

100 gm (each) pumpkin, tomatoes and onion

2 sprigs parsley

2 (each) peppercorns and bay leaves

1 clove garlic

2 vegetable stock cubes

2 tbsp salt

Method

Heat the oil in a large pan over moderate heat and add all the ingredients along with 6 cups of water and stir once it comes to a boil; simmer for 30 minutes. Liquidize and strain into a bowl and set aside until used. Makes 6 cups

Carrot and Lemon Soup

Ingredients

2 tbsp olive oil

1 medium onion, finely chopped

1 kg carrots, peeled and chopped

3½ cups Vegetable Stock (Page 245)

Grated rind and juice of 1 lemon

½ tsp (each) salt and pepper

2 tbsp chopped fresh parsley

Method

Heat olive oil in a saucepan; sauté onion and carrots for 5-7 minutes stirring occasionally. Cook until vegetables are soft. Stir in the stock, lemon juice, lemon rind, salt and pepper. Bring to a boil and simmer for 25 minutes. Remove from stove and set aside to cool.

Purée the mixture in the blender, sieve and return to heat. Garnish with parsley and serve.

Serves } 4

Russian Salad Deluxe

Ingredients

1 cup Mayonnaise (Page 244)

1 cup grated Cheddar cheese

1 tbsp mustard

200 gm tinned green asparagus tips

2 cups mixed boiled vegetables (carrots, peas, potatoes, French beans and yellow corn kernels)

Salt and pepper to taste

To garnish
A few lettuce leaves and sliced olives

To serve
Melba Toast (recipe follows)

Method

Mix together the mayonnaise, grated cheese and mustard in a medium bowl. Add asparagus tips, boiled vegetables, salt and pepper and mix well. Chill until ready to serve.

To serve, transfer to a serving bowl lined with lettuce leaves; garnish with olives and serve with Melba toast.

Serves | 6

Melba Toast

Cut any kind of bread into thin slices (small or big). Bake in a hot oven until crisp (approx 20 minutes).

Salade Gourmande

French Beans Salad

Ingredients

200 gm (each) French beans topped and tailed, and baby potatoes

For the dressing

2 tsp (each) olive oil, sesame oil, lemon juice, cider vinegar, finely-chopped tarragon, parsley and chives

Salt and pepper to taste

To garnish

A few salad greens

Slivers of Parmesan cheese and almonds

Finely-chopped spring onions

Note: You may divide the vegetables into 4 portions.

Method

Cook French beans in plenty of salted water until *al dente*. Remove beans with slotted spoon and plunge them in cold water for 10 seconds. Drain thoroughly. Wash and boil the baby potatoes in salted water, peel and cut into halves. Toss beans and potatoes separately with the dressing.

For the dressing

Place all the ingredients for the dressing in a small bowl and whisk together until mixed well. Set aside.

To serve

Place a few leaves of salad greens on serving plate, and arrange tossed beans over in a criss-cross pattern. Sprinkle a little of the spring onions. Pile up potatoes on top and garnish with spring onions, slivered Parmesan and almonds.

Serves } 4

Red Pepper and Beans Salad

Ingredients

150 gm dried white beans, soaked overnight and boiled

1 medium red capsicum, sliced

250 gm French beans, cut into 2" pieces and blanched

½ cup sliced black olives

For the dressing

¼ cup olive oil

2 tsp (each) grated rind of lemon and dried mixed herbs

2 tbsp wine vinegar

1 tbsp (each) balsamic vinegar and Dijon mustard

Salt and pepper to taste

To garnish

Bed of lettuce and slivered and toasted almonds

To serve

Crusty bread brushed with sesame-flavoured butter

Method

For the dressing

Blend all the ingredients in a small liquidizer jar.

Place the vegetables, olives and beans in a bowl and toss them with the dressing. Cover and chill in refrigerator for 1-2 hours. Garnish and serve with crusty bread.

Serves } 6-8

Asparagus Mousse

Ingredients

1 tin (425 gm) green or white asparagus tips

1 tbsp unflavoured gelatine

1 vegetable stock cube, crumbled

1 cup grated Cheddar cheese

2 tbsp Mayonnaise (Page 244)

2 cloves garlic (optional)

Salt, pepper and mustard to taste

200 gm fresh cream

To garnish

A few lettuce leaves, freshly chopped chives and 1 or 2 asparagus tips

Method

Drain the asparagus tips and reserve the liquid.

Soak gelatine in ¼ cup of the liquid mixed with the stock cube. Cook gently until melted, and set aside to cool.

Place asparagus tips, cheese, mayonnaise, garlic, salt, pepper and mustard in a liquidiser jar. Blend until smooth. With the motor running, gradually add the cooled gelatine mixture, making sure each addition is absorbed well before adding the next.

Transfer to a large bowl. Beat the cream over ice until thick. Fold into the asparagus mixture and transfer to a 4-cup capacity bowl or mould and place in a refrigerator or freeze until set. Unmould on to a plate, arrange lettuce leaves around and garnish with chives and asparagus tips.

Serves } 6-8

French Onion Toast

Ingredients

2 tbsp butter

2 tbsp olive oil

6 medium onions, halved and thinly sliced

2 tsp powdered sugar

Salt and pepper to taste

250 ml white wine or Vegetable Stock (Page 245), or half of each

4-6 half inch-thick slices of French bread (baguette)

2 tbsp mustard

100 gm Gruyère cheese, grated

Method

Melt butter and oil in a heavy frying pan; add onions and cook gently for 20 minutes, tossing occasionally, until soft. Add sugar, salt and pepper and cook for another 10 minutes until golden brown. Increase the heat and add the wine or stock and allow to bubble for 1 minute. Reduce heat and cook for 5 minutes or until the liquid is absorbed.

Heat the grill or the oven and toast the bread slices. Spread mustard evenly on each one. Pile the onions on top and sprinkle with cheese. Place under the grill for 1-2 minutes until golden brown. Serve hot.

Serves } 4-6

Vol-au-Vent de Champignon et Broccoli

Mushroom and Broccoli in Puff Pastry

Ingredients

2 tbsp butter

1 medium onion, finely chopped

2 cloves garlic, crushed

300 gm fresh mushrooms, washed and cut into cubes

250 gm broccoli florets, washed and blanched

50 gm walnuts, chopped and toasted

Salt and pepper to taste

For golden roux

3 tbsp butter

6 tbsp plain flour

½ cup white wine (optional)

2 cups Vegetable Stock (Page 245)

Salt, pepper and nutmeg to taste

¼ cup fresh cream

1 large or 12 medium vol-au-vent shells

To garnish

Sprigs of parsley and grated cheese

Method

Melt butter in a heavy saucepan; sauté onion, garlic and mushrooms and cook until soft. Add broccoli, walnuts, salt and pepper. Set aside.

For golden roux

Heat butter in a small saucepan; add flour and wine (if using) and cook until it changes colour. Remove from stove and add the stock. Mix well to get a smooth mixture. Return to the stove and add salt, pepper, nutmeg and cream. Bring to a boil and simmer until thick.

Cut the top of the vol-au-vent/s and set aside to use as lid/s. Remove the soft pastry from the centre and bake it in a hot oven to make it crisp. Mix the roux with the mushroom mixture and fill the vol-au-vent shell/s. Cover with the lid/s; place it on a serving plate. Garnish with parsley sprigs and grated cheese. Serve immediately.

Serves } 6

Vegetable and Cheese Pie

Ingredients

500 gm mixed vegetables, cut into cubes and boiled

2 bunches spinach (approx. 250 gm), washed, boiled and puréed

100 gm cottage cheese

100 gm chopped onion

100 gm Cheddar cheese

Salt and pepper to taste

For the cheese sauce

¼ cup butter

¼ cup plain flour

1½ cups milk

Salt, pepper and mustard to taste

½ cup grated Cheddar cheese

For the creamed potatoes

½ kg potatoes

1 tbsp milk

1 tbsp butter

Salt to taste

To garnish

Chopped parsley

Method

For the cheese sauce
Melt butter in a thick saucepan; stir in the flour and cook, stirring continuously for 2-3 minutes. Remove from heat and add the milk, stirring continuously. Return to heat, add the seasonings and cheese and bring to a boil. Take the pan off the heat and set aside.

Makes 2 cups

For the creamed potatoes
Boil the potatoes. Drain, peel and mash until soft. While the potatoes are still hot, add the milk and beat with a wooden spoon until white and fluffy. Add the butter and salt.

To assemble the pie
Grease a round or square 6-cup capacity baking dish with a little butter. Mix the cheese sauce with the vegetables, reserving 2 tbsp for the spinach. Pour the vegetable mixture into the dish.

In a small bowl, mix together spinach, cottage cheese, onion, salt, pepper and 2 tbsp cheese sauce. Spread the mixture over the vegetables. Sprinkle with grated cheese. Spread two-third of the creamed potatoes on top. Fill the remaining potato mixture in a piping bag and pipe a border of mashed potato around the rim of the dish. Bake in a hot oven at 400°F/200°C/Gas Mark 6 for 20 minutes. Garnish with chopped parsley and serve hot.

Serves } 6-8

Potatoes Niçoise

Potatoes Layered with Onions and Tomatoes

Ingredients

1 large clove garlic

2 tbsp finely-chopped parsley

1 tsp finely-chopped basil

1 tsp finely-chopped tarragon

1 tsp finely-chopped chives

450 gm potatoes, thickly sliced

3 tsp salt

1½ tsp pepper powder

¼ tsp nutmeg

450 gm onions, thinly sliced

500 gm large tomatoes, blanched and thickly sliced

2-3 tbsp butter

½ cup grated Gruyère or any other sharp cheese

Method

Preheat the oven to 400°F/200°C/Gas Mark 6. Rub an 8-9-inch round ovenproof dish with the cut clove of garlic.

In a small bowl, combine parsley, basil, tarragon and chives. Arrange a layer of potatoes in the dish and sprinkle with herbs, salt, pepper and nutmeg. Add a layer of onions, and then tomatoes and sprinkle with salt. Repeat the layers, ending with tomatoes. Dot the top with butter, cover and bake for 45 minutes or until potatoes are tender. Sprinkle the top with cheese and bake for 5 more minutes to brown the top slightly.

Serve hot as an accompaniment to a French meal.

Serves } 6

See Italian section

Pizza Tartlets (recipe on page 54)

Popcorn Soup (recipe on page 43)

Panini (recipe on page 50)

Asparagus Charlotte

Ingredients

1 kg fresh asparagus

½ cup (each) finely-chopped spring onion, red and yellow capsicums

2 medium tomatoes, peeled and chopped

¼ cup butter

½ cup (each) fresh cream and cheese of your choice

1 tbsp (each) crushed garlic and chopped herbs

2 tbsp cornflour

1 stock cube mixed with ¼ cup hot water

8 slices white bread, sides removed and buttered

2-3 tbsp milk

7″ round loose-bottomed tin or 6 small ramekin dishes

For tomato cream sauce

1 cup tomatoes, grilled, puréed and sieved

1 tbsp (each) butter, shallots and fresh cream

1 tsp cider vinegar

1 sprig (¼ tsp) fresh thyme

Salt and pepper to taste

For onion compote

100 gm small onions, peeled and blanched

1 tbsp (each) butter and sugar

½ tsp (each) paprika, parsley, black pepper and salt

2 tbsp toasted and chopped almonds

To garnish

Dried tomato peel, chopped chives and filo pastry cup

Method

Trim the asparagus; cut top part of the tips to match the height of the tin or ramekin dish. Cut the rest into small pieces. Cook both in boiling water until tender. Purée the small cut asparagus in the blender and set aside. Melt butter in a heavy frying pan and sauté garlic, spring onion and capsicums for 2 minutes. Add the tomatoes, asparagus purée and vegetable stock mixed with cornflour. Cook until mixture becomes thick. Add cream, cheese and herbs. Mix well. Remove from fire and set aside to cool.

For tomato cream sauce

Melt butter in a saucepan and sauté shallots and thyme until soft. Add tomatoes, vinegar, salt and pepper. Remove from stove and add the cream. Keep warm.

For onion compote

Melt butter in a small pan; add onions and sugar and cook until sugar caramelises. Add salt, pepper, parsley and paprika. Cook until thick. Fold in the almonds once it is cold.

To assemble

Line the tin or ramekin dishes with bread slices and sprinkle with milk. Set aside for 5-10 minutes. Gently pour in the asparagus mixture and bake in moderate oven at 325°F/170°C/ Gas Mark 3, for 15-20 minutes or until mixture is set. Remove from oven and allow it to cool slightly. Unmould the charlotte on a serving plate over a pool of tomato cream sauce. Arrange asparagus tips around the border of the dish inside of the bread lining. Garnish charlotte with onion compote and dried tomato peel. Place additional compote at the side on the plate in filo pastry cup. Sprinkle chopped chives all over. Serve warm.

Serves } 6

French Bread with Homemade Boursin

Ingredients

1 loaf French bread, cut into ½ inch-thick slices

2-3 tbsp butter

For boursin

225 gm cream cheese

2 tbsp (each) sour cream and softened butter

1 tbsp (each) freshly chopped parsley and chives

½ tsp (each) chopped marjoram, salt and white pepper

1 large clove garlic, minced

1 tbsp grated Parmesan cheese

Method

Butter bread slices, wrap them in foil and set aside. Bake in hot oven 10 minutes before serving.

Boursin

Beat cream cheese, butter and sour cream with an electric beater until fluffy. Add salt, pepper and garlic and beat until well mixed. Fold in the remaining ingredients and mix till they are properly blended.

Line 2-3 small tins or moulds with foil. Fill them with boursin and chill until ready to use. This cheese keeps fresh in the refrigerator for 8-10 days.

Makes 250 gm

Note: Use this as a spread for breads, as a dip, as garnish for soups etc.

Corn and Potato Rösti

Ingredients

4 tbsp butter

1 medium onion chopped

1 green chilli, finely chopped

4 medium potatoes, peeled and coarsely grated

¾ cup yellow corn kernels, boiled or tinned

2 tbsp grated Cheddar cheese

Salt and pepper to taste

Method

Heat butter in a thick frying pan and add onion. Cook for 1-2 minutes.

In a bowl toss together potatoes, corn, salt and pepper. Lower the heat and spread potato and corn mixture evenly over the onions in the frying pan. Sprinkle chilli and cheese on top. Cover the pan with a lid and cook for 10 minutes. Turn over the rösti without breaking it. Cook the other side until crisp.

Transfer rösti on a serving plate, cut into wedges and serve hot.

Serves } 4

Asparagus and Parmesan on Potato Rösti

Ingredients

500 gm potatoes, peeled and grated

100 gm butter

8-10 pieces fresh or tinned asparagus tips

¼ cup grated Parmesan cheese

Salt and pepper to taste

For parsley sauce

2 tbsp finely chopped parsley

1 cup (each) milk and Quick Vegetable Stock (recipe follows)

2 tbsp (each) butter and plain flour

3 tbsp thick cream

Salt and pepper to taste

Method

For the sauce
Blend half the stock along with parsley in a blender. Melt butter in a saucepan; add the flour and cook for 1-2 minutes. Add parsley-flavoured stock and stir until smooth. Whisk in the milk and remaining stock. Return the pan to the stove and allow it to boil until thick, stirring from time to time. Stir in the cream, salt and pepper. Heat gently. Keep warm.

For the rösti
Melt 2 tbsp butter in a heavy frying pan; Drain the potatoes completely and pat dry. Take a fistful and place on the side of the pan. Similarly place 4-5 dollops of potatoes at a time. Cover and cook on slow fire. Turn over when golden brown and cook the other side. Repeat until all the potato is used. Transfer the rösti onto a greased baking dish and keep warm.

Cut asparagus into 1" pieces. Boil if using fresh ones and drain if using tinned ones. Toss them with Parmesan cheese, salt and pepper. Spoon a few tips on each rösti, top with parsley sauce and bake for 4-5 minutes. Serve at once.

Quick Vegetable Stock
Immerse one stock cube in one cup of boiling water and stir till cube dissolves.

Serves | 6

Bread-crusted Vegetable Pot Pie

Ingredients

3-4 slices wholewheat bread

1+2 tbsp softened butter

1 medium onion and tomato, finely chopped

2 medium (each) carrots, potatoes and zucchini cut into cubes

200 gm (each) mushrooms, cut into cubes and shelled peas

¼ cup wholewheat flour

1 cup (each) milk and Vegetable Stock (Page 245)

200 gm crumbled cottage cheese

¼ cup (each) finely-chopped parsley and chives

1 tbsp cider vinegar

½ tsp (each) chilli flakes and garlic salt

⅓ cup grated Parmesan cheese

Salt and pepper to taste

To garnish

A bunch of parsley

To serve

Dijon mustard

Method

Cut each bread slice diagonally, spread 1 tbsp butter on each triangle and arrange around the edge of a 9-inch pie dish.

In a medium skillet, melt remaining butter and sauté onion, carrots and zucchini until soft. Add potatoes, mushrooms and tomato. Season with salt and pepper. Cook until mushroom shrinks a bit. Sprinkle the flour over the vegetables and stir to coat. Cook for 2-3 minutes. Carefully add the stock and milk, stirring constantly. Simmer and cook over medium heat until slightly thickened. Remove from heat and cool slightly.

In a small bowl, mix together herbs, peas, vinegar, chilli flakes, garlic salt and pepper. Pour cooled vegetable mixture into bread-lined pie dish spreading evenly. Cover the top with cottage cheese and sprinkle with Parmesan cheese. Bake in preheated oven at 350°F/180°C/ Gas Mark 4 for 30 minutes. Garnish with parsley and serve with mustard.

Serves } 8

Tomato Jam and Feta Cheese Slice

Ingredients

2 cups plain flour, sieved

1 tsp (each) baking powder and salt

3 tbsp butter

½ cup milk

For the filling

3 tbsp butter

1 small onion finely chopped

100 gm crumbled feta cheese mixed with 1 tsp corn flour

5-6 fresh basil leaves, torn into pieces

½ cup Tomato Jam (recipe follows)

For tomato jam

3 tbsp olive oil

1 medium onion, sliced thinly

6 large tomatoes, blanched, deseeded and chopped

5 pieces sun-dried tomatoes, soaked and chopped

4 tbsp brown sugar

1 tsp (each) wine vinegar and oregano

For garnish

1 cup grated Cheddar cheese

Chilli flakes

Method

Tomato Jam

Heat oil in a pan and add onion; sauté until transparent. Add the tomatoes, sugar, oregano and vinegar. Cover and cook for 25-30 minutes, until tomatoes and onions are broken down and the mixture has a jam-like consistency. Cover and set aside to cool.
Makes 1 cup

For the filling

Heat butter in a frying pan, add onions and cook until translucent. Remove from stove and add ½ cup tomato jam, feta cheese and basil. Use as required.

Sieve flour with baking powder and salt. Rub butter into sifted flour; add enough milk to make soft dough. Knead the dough on a floured surface. Divide the dough into two portions. Roll out one portion and place it on greased 9"x11" Swiss roll tin. Spread with filling. Cover with remaining portion of rolled out dough. Sprinkle with cheese, mark into squares by cutting through top layer of the dough. Bake in a hot oven at 350°F/180°C/Gas Mark 4 for 20-30 minutes or until golden brown. Sprinkle with chilli flakes. Place on wire rack, cut into squares and serve hot or cold.

Makes 24 pieces

Spinach and Cottage Cheese Bread Bowl

Ingredients

10 pieces 4 inch-round or 3 pieces of 6 inch-round crusty bread

2 bunches (250 gm) spinach leaves, chopped

2-3 tbsp butter

1 medium (each) red capsicum and onion, finely chopped

2 cups crumbled cottage cheese

4-5 cheese slices cut into pieces

2 tbsp tomato sauce

1 tbsp dried mixed herbs

Salt and pepper to taste

Olive oil to brush

To serve

Herb-flavoured Sauce (recipe follows)

Method

Slice off the tops of the bread loaves and reserve. Scoop out inside of the loaves leaving a thin shell. Brush the shells with olive oil and toast them slightly in a hot oven.

Drop spinach into pan of boiling water for one minute and drain. Sauté onion and red capsicum in 2 tbsp melted butter until tender. Add spinach, salt and pepper. Fill each of the loaves with the spinach mixture, leaving the centre empty.

In a small bowl mix together cottage cheese, tomato sauce, herbs, salt and pepper. Fill centre of each loaf with this mixture. Spread the cheese slice pieces on top, wrap the loaf in foil and bake it in a hot oven for 10-15 minutes. Remove from oven and let it stand for 5 minutes. Open the foil and transfer to a serving plate, half cover it with the lid that was sliced from the bread and serve with herb-flavoured sauce.

Herb-flavoured Sauce

Make Cheese Sauce (Page 74). Add 2 tbsp freshly chopped herbs (parsley, basil, chives, oregano etc).

Serves } 6

Rice and Vegetables in Creamy Sauce

Ingredients

2 cups thick-grained rice, washed and soaked

1 stock cube

2 tbsp butter

2 cups vegetables of your choice, boiled or grilled

For the sauce

2 tbsp butter

½ cup finely-chopped onion

2 cloves garlic, crushed

1 tbsp plain flour

1 cup (each) milk and cream

1 tbsp freshly chopped herbs

½ cup grated cheese

Salt, pepper and chilli flakes to taste

To serve

1 cup toasted bread croutons

¼ cup spiced olive oil

½ cup (each) soaked and chopped sun-dried tomatoes and finely-chopped spring onions

½ cup potato sticks

Method

Cook the rice in 4 cups of boiling water to which 1 stock cube is added until rice is cooked yet firm. Remove from stove and toss with butter, vegetables, salt and pepper. Keep warm.

For the sauce

Heat butter in a thick saucepan; add onion and garlic and cook until soft. Add plain flour and cook for 2 minutes. Remove from stove and add milk and cream mixing well. Return to stove and bring to a boil, stirring all the time until slightly thick. Simmer the sauce and add herbs, cheese, salt, pepper and chilli flakes. Place pan over a small burner, keeping the sauce hot.

To serve

Place rice at the bottom of individual bowls and ladle the sauce over it. Garnish with croutons, olive oil, sun-dried tomato, spring onion and potato sticks. Allow your guests to make their own mixture.

Serves } 6-8

Desserts

Here are some delectable desserts that are a fitting finale to any meal. Sugar, milk, butter, flour, chocolate, cream, dried fruits and ice cream come together in perfect harmony to create these marvellous sweet endings! Scrumptious Date and Almond Wontons, smooth and silky Chocolate Velvet Pie, a fusion surprise called Banoffee Pie and White Chocolate and Strawberry Mousse to die for!

Date and Almond Wontons

Ingredients

20 wonton wrappers

2 tbsp powdered sugar

1 tbsp cinnamon powder

¼ cup milk

Oil for frying

For the filling

½ cup (each) finely chopped dates and brown sugar

2-3 tbsp (each) toasted sesame seeds and chopped almonds

1 tbsp butter

To serve

Vanilla ice cream

Method

For the filling

Slightly crush the sesame seeds and mix them with dates, sugar, almonds and butter. Set aside.

Place 1 tsp of filling in the centre of wonton wrapper. Lift up opposite edges and stick them together with the help of milk and then bring the corners together to form a hat-shaped wonton. Repeat this for the rest of the wontons and deep-fry in oil until golden. Drain on kitchen paper.

Sprinkle a little sugar and cinnamon on each one and serve hot with vanilla ice cream.

Makes 20 wontons

White Chocolate and Strawberry Mousse

Ingredients

For the syrup

1/3 cup chopped strawberries

2 tbsp sugar

1 ½ tbsp cornflour

For the mousse

600 gm strawberries, washed and stemmed

½-¾ cup powdered sugar

1 tbsp lemon juice

200 gm white chocolate, cut into pieces

2 cups whipping cream

½ cup powdered or icing sugar

1 tsp vanilla essence

To garnish

2-3 whole strawberries and chocolate shavings

Method

For the syrup

Sprinkle 2 tbsp sugar over 1/3 cup chopped strawberries and set aside for 5 minutes. Strain to obtain 1/3 cup syrup by slightly mashing strawberries. Sprinkle cornflour over the syrup and mix well to get rid of the lumps. Set aside.

For the mousse

Purée 600 gm strawberries in a liquidizer jar. The strawberry pulp should measure approximately 2 1/3 cups. Place the pulp, sugar, lemon juice and cornflour mixture in a saucepan over medium heat. Cook gently until sugar melts and the mixture becomes slightly thick. Remove from stove and add white chocolate. Stir till chocolate has melted.

Transfer this to a steel bowl, and chill over ice, stirring often.

In another stainless steel bowl beat the cream with sugar and vanilla. Fold this into strawberry mixture. Pour the mixture into a serving bowl. Garnish with halved strawberries and chocolate shavings.

Serves } 6-8

Lemon and Pineapple Ice Cream

Ingredients

1 tin (450 gm) pineapple slices

¾ cup sugar

1 tbsp gelatine

3 tbsp lemon juice

½ litre milk, boiled and cooled

2 cups fresh cream, beaten

Method

Liquidise pineapple slices with the syrup. Mix sugar and gelatine powder along with pineapple pulp. Heat the mixture till gelatine and sugar dissolve. Remove from fire and cool. Add lemon juice and milk. Place this over a bowl of ice cubes and beat with an egg beater. When the mixture begins to set, add the cream and continue beating till all the cream is incorporated.

Either freeze it in a metal box or churn it in an ice cream machine.

Serves } 8

Note: You can garnish the ice cream with freshly chopped pineapple pieces when serving.

Banoffee Pie

Ingredients

For the crust

1 1/3 cup plain flour, sieved

½ cup cold butter, cut into cubes

¼ cup powdered sugar

3-4 tbsp thick cream

½ tsp salt

For the filling

1 tin (400 gm) sweetened condensed milk

¼ cup butter

3-4 medium ripe bananas, peeled and thinly sliced

1 tbsp lemon juice

For the topping

1 cup whipping cream

½ tsp instant coffee powder

1-2 tbsp (each) icing sugar and toasted flaked almonds

Method

For the crust
Combine flour, salt and sugar in a bowl; add cold butter cut into cubes and rub with the fingertips into the flour to resemble breadcrumbs. Add cream and mix lightly to form a ball. Add little cold water if required. Cover the dough and place in the fridge for 10 minutes. Remove and roll out to 9-10 inch round circle and press this into an 8-inch pie dish. Prick it with a fork and cover with foil. Place in the freezer for 30 minutes. Remove and bake in hot oven at 350°F/180°C/Gas Mark 4 for 20 minutes. Set aside.

For the filling
Bring lots of water to a boil in a large saucepan; simmer and immerse the tin of condensed milk in it, sideways. Boil for 3 hours. Remove the can and cool.

In another saucepan, melt ¼ cup butter and add boiled and cooled condensed milk and cook for 5 minutes, stirring constantly. Remove from fire and mix well. Leave to cool slightly.

Arrange sliced banana on the pastry case. Drizzle with lemon juice. Pour warm toffee over and set aside to cool.

For the topping
Whip the cream in a stainless steel bowl over ice with icing sugar until soft peaks form. Swirl the cream over toffee to cover the whole surface. Chill until required. Sprinkle flaked almonds and instant coffee just before serving.

Serves } 8-10

Fruit and Praline Sundae

Ingredients

For the sundae

500 gm nougat ice cream

1 cup chopped fruits

1 cup praline sauce (recipe follows)

For the praline sauce

¼ cup butter

½ cup brown sugar

2 tbsp maple syrup or honey

¼ cup water

1 tsp rum or brandy (optional)

½ cup finely-chopped nuts (almonds, walnuts, cashew nuts, or a mixture of all three)

Method

Semi-soften the ice cream and divide amongst individual glasses or press it down in a transparent bowl. Freeze it overnight if possible.

For the sauce
Heat butter over medium heat until golden, and cool. Gradually add sugar, mixing until smooth. Stir in maple syrup and water. Bring to boil and stir for 1 minute. Cool slightly, and then stir in the rum/brandy (if using) and nuts. Keep warm.

To assemble
Layer sliced fruits over frozen ice cream and pour warm sauce over the fruits just before serving.

Serves } 4–6

Fruit and Praline Sundae

Date and Almond Wontons
(recipe on page 236)

Peach Cobbler

Ingredients

3 cups peeled and sliced fresh peaches

½ cup granulated sugar

¼ cup (each) cold butter cut into cubes and slivered almonds

A pinch of cinnamon powder

For the top crust

1 cup plain flour, sieved

2 tsp baking powder

1 tbsp granulated sugar

1 tsp salt

¼ cup butter

½ cup thick cream

To serve

Vanilla ice cream

Method

Arrange sliced fresh peaches in the bottom of a buttered 6-cup capacity baking dish. Sprinkle with ½ cup sugar and cinnamon. Dot the peaches with ¼ cup butter which has been cut into small pieces. Preheat the oven to 375°F/190°C/Gas Mark 5.

For the crust, mix together flour, baking powder, 1 tablespoon sugar, and salt. Cut in the remaining ¼ cup butter. Stir in the cream until dough is manageable. Roll out dough on a lightly floured surface to fit on top of the baking dish over the sliced peaches. Bake in the preheated oven for 35 minutes, or till the top is nicely browned. Cut into wedges and serve hot with vanilla ice cream.

Serves } 6

Chocolate Velvet Pie

Ingredients

For the base

12-14 chocolate biscuits crushed into crumbs

1 tbsp melted butter

For the filling

300 gm chocolate chips or cooking chocolate cut into pieces

200 gm Philadelphia cream cheese, softened

1 tsp vanilla essence

1 cup whipping cream, whipped

To garnish

Sweetened whipped cream and mint/ chocolate chips

Method

For the base
Mix biscuit crumbs with butter and press into an 8" pie dish. Set aside.

For the filling
Melt the chocolate in a microwave oven for 1 minute or place over a pan of hot water until melted. Cool to room temperature.

In a medium-sized bowl beat cream cheese, sugar, vanilla and melted and cooled chocolate. Fold in whipped cream and spoon over the prepared base. Refrigerate for at least 2 hours or until firm.

Garnish with whipped cream and mint or chocolate chips. Cut into wedges and serve cold.

Serves } 8

Oreo Milkshake

Ingredients

3 pieces Oreo cookies

1 cup cold milk

1 scoop vanilla ice cream

2-3 drops vanilla essence

Sugar to taste

2-3 ice cubes

To garnish

Whipped cream, 1-2 crushed cookies

Method

Crush the cookies and set aside a few pieces for garnishing. Put the remaining ingredients in a liquidizer jar and process till well-blended. Pour out in a tall glass and garnish with whipped cream and crushed cookies. Serve immediately.

Serves } 1

Mayonnaise

Ingredients

1 egg

½ tsp (each) salt, pepper, mustard and sugar

2 tbsp vinegar or lemon juice

½ - ¾ cup salad oil

Method

Place the egg, salt, pepper, mustard and sugar in a liquidizer jar and blend at medium speed. When it is thoroughly blended, add oil in a very thin stream, now blending at high speed. DO NOT add oil too quickly or else the mayonnaise will curdle. After it has thickened, add vinegar or lemon juice and continue blending until mixed completely. Taste and adjust the seasoning. Store in an airtight container.

Makes 1 cup

VARIATIONS

Add 2 cloves of garlic while blending the mayonnaise to make garlic mayonnaise or aioli. Add 1 tsp curry powder and 2 tbsp finely-chopped onions to make curry mayonnaise.

Eggless Mayonnaise

Ingredients

200 gm fresh cream

2 tsp dry mustard powder

½ tsp (each) salt and pepper

2 tbsp sugar

2 tbsp white vinegar or lemon juice

¼ cup salad oil

Method

In a stainless steel bowl, combine fresh cream with mustard, salt, pepper and sugar. Put this over a bowl of crushed ice and beat with a beater until thick. Gradually add the oil till it gets completely absorbed in the cream. Add vinegar or lemon juice and chill until ready to serve.

Makes 1½ cups

Potato Mayonnaise

Ingredients

1 small potato, baked

1 tsp powdered sugar

1 tsp mustard

2 tbsp vinegar

1 tsp salt

¾ cup olive oil or salad oil

Method

Peel and mash the potato. Add mustard, salt and powdered sugar; add 1 tbsp vinegar, and rub mixture through a fine sieve. Beat the mixture with electric beater or put it in a blender. Slowly add oil and remaining vinegar.

Makes 1 cup

Vegetable Stock

Ingredients

2 medium onions, chopped

1 medium (each) leek and carrot, chopped

1 large sprig parsley tied with 1 bay leaf

1 small piece bottle gourd, chopped

6 cups water

Method

Put all the ingredients in the pressure cooker and cook for 3 whistles. Cool and discard the bay leaf and parsley bunch, then liquidise, sieve and set aside.

Makes 4–5 cups

Sour Cream

Mix together ½ cup thick yogurt, ¼ cup fresh cream and 1 tbsp of lemon juice.

Glossary

Al dente	Cooked until it offers just slight resistance to bite
Appetiser	A first course of a meal of tidbits, drinks or cocktails
Baguette	A long, thin loaf of French bread
Barbecue	To cook on a rack over a charcoal fire or gas
Basil	Fresh or dried, broken or ground leaves with pungent flavour and sweet aroma
Bay leaf	Dry leaf with strong flavour used whole or crushed
Bean curd	Tofu or soybean cake
Bell pepper/Pepper	Capsicum
Bird's eye chilli	Small, very hot chilli used in Southeast Asian cuisine
Boursin	Soft, creamy French cheese
Castor Sugar	Refined white sugar
Charlotte	A dish with a savoury or sweet filling baked in a mould
Cheddar	A hard, yellow cheese originally made in Cheddar, England
Compote	Fruit or vegetables stewed or cooked in sugar syrup
Chipotle	Smoke-dried jalapeño chilli used mainly in Mexican cuisine
Chives	Herb with long spiky green leaves, related to the onion
Chowder	A thick American-style soup
Cinnamon	Reddish brown stick of rolled bark with sweet pungent aroma
Condensed milk	Evaporated milk to which sugar has been added
Coriander	Whole seeds or fresh leaves with slightly orange flavour and aroma.
Crudités	A variety of fresh raw vegetables cut long and served ice-cold with a dip or by itself
Croûtons	Small pieces of bread, fried or toasted
Cumin	Whole seeds or ground with strong and slightly bitter flavour.
Curry powder	A blend of many spices giving a distinctive flavour
Feta	Greek cheese made from a mixture of sheep's and goat's milk
Fondue	A dish cooked on the table usually over a spirit heater. A Swiss fondue is of melted cheese and wine served with chunks of bread
Galangal	Thai variety of ginger

Gelatine	Unflavoured jelly crystals used to set the mixture
Ginger	Whole roots fresh or dried, pungent or hot
Gruyère	Hard, yellow Swiss cheese with a sharp taste
Jalapeño peppers	Spicy Mexican chillies of green variety
Kaffir lime leaves	Leaves of Thai lime tree, used for flavouring in Thai food
Lemon grass	Citrus-flavoured herb used in teas, soups and curries
Marinate	A seasoned liquid usually a blend of oil, wine, vinegar and seasonings to coat food and add flavour
Marjoram	Fresh or dried leaves with spicy, slightly bitter flavour
Mint	Fresh or dried leaves with strong, sweet aroma and cool after-taste
Monterey Jack	Tangy Mexican cheese
Mozzarella	Special tangy Italian cheese widely used for pizzas etc
MSG	Monosodium Glutamate, a seasoning often used to flavour Chinese food.
Nutmeg	Large whole seeds or ground with warm sweet aromatic flavour
Oregano	Dried or fresh leaves with strong flavour
Palm sugar	Unrefined brown sugar
Parmesan	A hard, grainy Italian cheese
Paprika	Spice made from dried bell peppers or capsicums
Parsley	Fresh leaves and stems with very strong flavour, similar to coriander
Pepper/peppercorn	Pungent spice used whole or powdered
Pine nuts	One of the popular nuts widely used in Middle-eastern cooking
Pita bread	Lebanese flat bread either made with plain flour or whole wheat
Praline	Sugar flavoured with coarsely-ground roasted nuts
Quiche	An open custard tart with savoury or sweet filling
Raw sugar	Unrefined white sugar
Rösti	Small Swiss pancakes made of raw grated potatoes
Roux	A thick sauce made with flour, butter and milk
Seasoning	Salt, pepper, spices, herbs etc., added to give depth of flavour
Shallots	Small onions with a sharp, pungent flavour
Simmer	To cook in a liquid at a temperature just below boiling point
Snow peas	A variety of Chinese peas eaten whole in its pod
Stir-fry	To cook quickly in a little oil stirring constantly
Stock	The liquid produced when vegetables are simmered in water for a long period to extract the flavour

Sun-dried tomatoes	Tomatoes that are dried in the sun for a number of days and then stored or preserved in olive oil
Tabasco sauce	Hot sauce made from Tabasco peppers and used in Mexican and American cuisine
Taco seasoning mix	A special blend of Mexican spice that is a combination of dried onion, garlic, chillies and other spices
Tahina/tahini	Sesame purée
Tamarind	Fruit of tamarind tree with sharp sour taste
Tarragon	Fresh or dried herb with sweet, aromatic and piquant flavour
Thyme	Fresh or dried or ground herb with pungent aromatic flavour
To bake	To cook in the oven by dry heat
To beat	A thin liquid mixed with an eggbeater to incorporate air and to thicken it gradually. This method is also used to make a mixture smooth and free from lumps
To blanch	To treat food with boiling water, loosen the skin and remove
To chill	To cool food without freezing in the refrigerator
To fry	To cook in hot oil
To fold in	To combine a light whisked mixture with other ingredients so that it retains its lightness
To grease	To coat the surface of a dish with fat to prevent sticking
To purée	To press food through a fine sieve in a blender or a food processor, to a smooth, thick mixture
To sauté	To cook in an open pan in hot, shallow fat, tossing the food to prevent sticking
To sieve	To rub or press moist or dry food through a sieve
To shred	To slice food into very thin pieces
To steam	To cook in the steam of boiling water without food touching water
To toss	Two or more ingredients mixed together without mashing with a fork
Tortilla	Thin, Mexican flat bread made with maize flour or plain flour
Tostada	Tortilla fried until crisp and served flat topped with beans or savoury mixture
Vichyssoise	Thick soup made of puréed vegetables, cream and stock
Vinaigrette	Salad dressing, sauce or marinade made of salad oil and vinegar with added seasoning
Vinegar	Generally made from malt, cider, sugarcane, red or white wine or grape juice to add sour taste to many dishes
Vol-au-vent	French for a small, hollow case of puff pastry
Wok	A Chinese cooking pan